EUROPE'S
NEXT
POWERHOUSE?

EUROPE'S NEXT POWERHOUSE?

THE EVOLUTION OF CHELSEA UNDER EMMA HAYES

A B D U L L A H   A B D U L L A H

Foreword by Suzanne Wrack

First published by Pitch Publishing, 2022

Pitch Publishing
A2 Yeoman Gate
Yeoman Way
Worthing
Sussex
BN13 3QZ
www.pitchpublishing.co.uk
info@pitchpublishing.co.uk

A CIP catalogue record is available for this book
from the British Library.

ISBN 978 1 80150 050 0

Typesetting and origination by Pitch Publishing
Printed and bound in Great Britain by TJ Books Ltd

Contents

Foreword   9

Preface   12

1. The Project   17

2. Emma Hayes   22

3. Build-up and Attacking Tactics   31

4. Role of the Forwards   51

5. Sam Kerr   61

6. Fran Kirby   76

7. Chelsea's Number 10 Role   92

8. Pernille Harder: The Modern Number 10?   97

9. Midfield Structure, Roles, and Problems   117

10. Ji So-yun   132

11. Melanie Leupolz   146

12. Sophie Ingle   160

13. Defensive Setup, Pressing and the Role of the Full-Backs   170

14. Magdalena Eriksson and Millie Bright   182

15. Maren Mjelde   202

16. Is the 3-4-2-1 Formation the Solution?   210

17. The Eleven   233

18. Can Chelsea Eclipse Lyon and Barcelona?   249

In memory of my loving grandmother. Your presence we miss, your memory we treasure. Loving you always.

Mum, Nunes, and Dad for their unwavering support.

Foreword

I GREW up in north London as an Arsenal fan. In many respects, as a young girl interested in football I was extremely lucky. Arsenal Women existed, were dominant and, at one stage, trained in the park opposite my council estate. When I went along to watch the double-winning parades there was the women's team on a bus behind the men's with their trophies in tow. Women's football was not abnormal, but it was far from normal too.

When I would trot around to the corner shop on the edge of our estate on Sunday mornings to pick up the newspapers for my dad, there was no women's football in the pages I would get leftover reading rights to. It was not on TV. The internet barely existed.

I had women's football in my line of sight more than most and yet my knowledge and awareness was still decidedly minimal.

Why am I discussing life as a young, female Arsenal fan in a book which picks apart and forensically examines how Chelsea Women have become one of the most dominant club teams in the women's game and taken themselves to the brink of European glory?

Quite simply because a book of this nature, one that analyses, discusses and explains the processes behind the building of Chelsea Women, speaks volumes to how far women's football has come. The very existence of this book is a part of the growing ecosystem around women's football and it is a big deal.

It also tells a story that needs to be told. Of how an extraordinary manager was given the time and space to construct a dynasty at a time when few other teams were as committed to the women's game. Emma Hayes herself has repeatedly said that one of her favourite aspects of managing the team is the tactical part. She delights in poring over the tactics board with her assistants for hours on end, working out exactly how she is to dissect the next opponent.

Ahead of Chelsea's Champions League semi-final against Lyon in 2019, Hayes gave myself and two other members of the press an insight into her analytical mind. In an hour-long session sat in her office she ran through the task at hand, pulling pieces across a tactics board as she rapid-fire reeled off who would be up against whom and how she would attempt to stop the seemingly unstoppable.

They failed. A 1-1 draw away was undone with a 2-1 defeat at home. Two years later, however, they would go a step further and reach the final of the competition only to suffer a crushing 4-0 defeat to Barcelona. There can be no doubting that Hayes has pored over that emphatic loss and is already well on her way to attempting to mastermind a way past the new European champions. Women's football fans revelled in being able to hear her in-game instructions during lockdown with stadiums empty, and a wider audience had a glimpse into her insane level of attention to detail through her punditry and co-commentary work during the men's Euros in 2021.

All the components that have gone into her Chelsea team reaching this point can be found within these pages. In many respects Abdullah Abdullah's book pays huge tribute to the manager who loves tactics by tactically analysing the way she has set up a team bidding to conquer Europe.

It also carves open a new corner of publishing on women's football. The small number of books devoted to the game have primarily been history books or biographies. Very few offer the reader an insight into the actual football itself and the nuances of the action on the pitch in the way this volume does. It will in turn go on to enrich the knowledge of fans, journalists, broadcasters, historians and coaches of a key team at a key moment in time. More critically, it broadens the space women's football occupies.

Suzanne Wrack

Preface

So remember me; I will remember you –
Surah Al-Baqarah (2:152)

Alhamdullilah

IT'S ASTONISHING for me to think that I'm releasing a second book in the space of 12 months. The thought of writing one still surprises me but two is almost unthinkable, yet here I am. Writing *Queens of Europe* was a dream come true – depicting a technical love letter to a team I am so deeply passionate about. When I contemplated the choices for a second book, there was really only one team I wanted to write about: Chelsea. I've supported the Blues since 2000, watching José Mourinho win back-to-back Premier League titles and both Roberto Di Matteo and Thomas Tuchel lift the Champions League trophy. Chelsea Football Club has been close to me for years and while I chose Lyon as my team in the women's game, I always wanted to do something around Chelsea so there was no better way to do it than through Chelsea Women.

They've proven their credentials by being serial winners and the prospect of depicting their journey was something that fascinated me and made me want to dedicate several thousand words towards showing you what they're all about. The basis of this book is to present the tactical concepts that have made them so successful, but also an opportunity to answer the ultimate question of whether they're ready to take that next step towards European domination.

I talked about a growing network in my first book and that has expanded even further now. Role models have become acquaintances and even friends, along with an ever-growing group of followers which has been incredibly humbling. I've met more astonishing people without forgetting my long-time friends (Domagoj, Lorihanna, Gavin, Ryan, and Daniel to name a few) who have stuck around even though life keeps us preoccupied. There are a few people to thank once again, all of whom played their part in making this book what it is.

First and foremost, I'd like to thank my family for their support and patience in giving me the time after work to finish chapter after chapter, night after night. I was privileged to speak to a few top-class personalities who were nothing short of spectacular and made me feel a part of the community. Let me introduce and thank the contributors below, in no particular order:

Suzanne Wrack, women's football writer for *The Guardian*: Suzy is responsible for the foreword but has also been a great source of advice and inspiration in helping me write this book, especially with her vast knowledge of Emma Hayes.

Om Arvind (founder of the *Tactical Rant* Substack, contributor to SB Nation's *Managing Madrid* podcast, and Real Madrid diehard): Om is a new member of the network but feels like someone I've known for years. He and I have been subject to numerous lengthy Zoom calls on tactical discussions on teams from the likes of Chelsea and Real Madrid, to Lyon and Sweden. His tactical knowledge was vital in affirming and learning more about tactical nuances.

Maram Al Baharna (senior player analyst and data consultant for Analytics FC), and Abhishek Sharma (data scientist and football consultant): I can't go by without mentioning the two G.O.A.T.s of data analysis. I wanted to take this book to another level and collaborating with two of the best in the business made sense when the opportunity arose. They were a tremendous help and all the visualisations you'll see are courtesy of these two.

Alex Ibaceta (journalist for BBC Sport) and Jessy Parker-Humphreys (freelance writer): A special shoutout to my two co-hosts and now friends, Alex 'Alexia' Ibaceta and Jessy 'Jessy' Parker-Humphreys, whom I do the *Box to Box WSL* podcast with. Our story began in November 2020 when we collaborated on a tactical webinar on Sarina Weigman's England side. This evolved into Alex inviting us to join her to revive her podcast. It's been an incredible journey and I'm grateful to have learned and earned their respect.

There are a few honourable mentions for Mia Eriksson (sports photographer and analyst), Jasmina Schweimler (VfL Wolfsburg expert and writer for *Sportbuzzer* and *WazWolfsburg*), Carlon Carpenter (Stats Bomb and Bath City FC analyst), Ameé Ruszkai (*Goal*'s women's football correspondent), Donna Newberry (women's football analyst), Antonio Maza aka NWSL Analitica (analyst at California Storm and scout at Houston Dash), Keiran Doyle (assistant coach, University of Toronto Women's Soccer), Sophie Lawson (women's football freelance writer), Matt Davies-Adams (commentator on Chelsea TV and podcaster), Liam Twomey (The Athletic's Chelsea reporter), and Louise Taffa (Australian football host/presenter and BBC Sport contributor).

I also have to give a special shoutout to the guys at the *London Is Blue* podcast. Nick Verlaney, Brandon Busbee, and Dan Dormer are three fantastic individuals who gave me a platform to start my own podcast on Chelsea Women alongside Jessy. *Blue Royalty* has been such an unbelievable platform to create content on and I can't thank them enough for the opportunity.

Lastly, my editor and childhood friend Ravshan Ergashev has been instrumental in making sure this book stayed on course and had a major assist all the way through the creative process. He is the man responsible for my improvement in writing, so thank you, my friend.

A lot has changed in the past 12 months, especially since the release of *Queens of Europe*. Along with two books, I've started my own Substack newsletter called *Pressing Matters*, written for Analytics FC, featured on UEFA's Women's Champions League Final preview show as a panellist, and worked for Houston Dash. It's incredible how things can change in a blink of an eye. Ten years ago I was starting university not knowing what I wanted to do in life and where it was going to take me and now I have a host of opportunities ahead of me. With that, I hope you enjoy reading this as much as I enjoyed writing it.

1

The Project

ON SUNDAY, 16 May 2021, the world was about to witness a new era emerge in Sweden. There was excitement, anxiety, and intrigue brewing in the air. For the first time in five years there was no sign of the 'Queens of Europe' (Olympique Lyonnais Féminin) in the UEFA Women's Champions League Final. It was a chance for a new team to engrave their name in European folklore and establish themselves as a new dominant force in the continent. For Barcelona Femení, it was a chance to avenge their humiliation of the 2019 final against Olympique Lyonnais and a reward for an incredible turnaround. For Chelsea, the final was an ascent that had been years in the making, supplemented by a most incredible season. Gothenburg was about to witness the start of greatness.

'This is the house Emma Hayes has built' –
Liam Twomey

Ever since Roman Abramovich bought Chelsea in 2003, he's turned the London club from mid-table mediocrity to serial champions. The change in fortunes may have come from the oligarch's immense riches, but he also brought a winning mentality that trickled from the top. Every manager who has taken charge of the men's team has brought some form of success, whether it be José Mourinho winning three Premier League titles, Carlo Ancelotti winning the Premier League and FA Cup double, or Thomas Tuchel delivering a second UEFA Champions League title. These coaches have created leaders in each of their squads. They had strong voices and tough personalities, but more importantly, they were players who propelled the team forward. John Terry, Frank Lampard, Michael Ballack, Petr Cech and Didier Drogba were the quintessential leaders of yesteryear who transferred this mentality from squad to squad until their inevitable swansong in 2012 that was capped with the club's first Champions League triumph.

There are many parallels you can draw between Chelsea's men's and women's teams, not least their insatiable desire to win. Ever since they were founded in 1992, Chelsea Women – or Chelsea Ladies as they were initially named – have had their own ups and downs. Between 2005 and 2010 they were fighting for their place in the FA Premier League National Division, even narrowly avoiding relegation in the 2005/06 season.

Soon after, they went through a couple of managerial changes and signed some top-class players in Siobhan

Chamberlain, Casey Stoney and Eniola Aluko. They even signed the United States player and World Cup winner Lorrie Fair, regarded then as one of the best midfielders in the women's game, in January of the 2007/08 season. This was the start of their upward trajectory.

After a fifth-place finish in 2007/08, Chelsea Ladies went on to finish third in 2008/09 behind Arsenal and Everton. The following season saw Aluko and Anita Asante leave for the new Women's Professional Soccer League (United States) in March 2009, while Fair missed the whole campaign with an unfortunate cruciate ligament injury sustained in May 2008. The manager Steve Jones then departed in January 2009, leaving Stoney to become a player/manager.

During the 2009/10 season, cuts to the team's funding were announced which threatened to derail the club but were then offset by the input of capital from John Terry and other Chelsea players. The club then appointed Matt Beard, on the recommendation of Stoney, who stayed on for three more years. Beard did well in his stint as manager and was there when Chelsea successfully bid to be one of eight founding teams in the Women's Super League in March 2011. While Beard took them to their first Women's FA Cup Final, it was the introduction of Emma Hayes in 2012 that kick-started the project. Though their first two seasons were underwhelming, a period of acclimatisation was necessary for Hayes to understand the needs and requirements of the squad. This signalled the beginning of Chelsea's most successful period and the first step towards them becoming European giants, though most couldn't see that happening at first.

'Thanks to the resources committed to this team by Mr Abramovich, Emma Hayes has been able to build this recently amateur side into a European giant with a roster of the biggest names in women's football.

'As fans, we are so lucky to be able to watch Emma build her vision both on and off the pitch. This group of women are such a bright spot that so many Chelsea fans are proud of. They consistently win trophies and do it the Chelsea way. We are so lucky to have the one-club mentality,' enthused Brandon Busbee.

In Hayes's first season in charge, Chelsea finished third-last in the league. The following season, they fared worse and unfortunately finished second from bottom. The 2014 season signalled the start of an incredible turnaround for the club, and they've managed to finish in the top three of the WSL every season since. They've been crowned champions four times since then, along with winning two Women's FA Cups and two Women's League Cups. In 2015, it was announced that many of Chelsea's players would be becoming full professionals for the first time, signalling the club's intent. Though it is ultimately the UEFA Women's Champions League that they are yet to capture, they've reached three semi-finals and one final in seven seasons.

The 2020/21 season was their opportunity to slay their demons and banish the ghosts of yesteryear by going through their best transfer window. Alas, it wasn't to be.

Barcelona thoroughly outplayed Chelsea, dominating them in every phase of play. This wasn't the Chelsea we had seen throughout the season, so the question arose: was this merely a blip, or is there more to it? For Hayes, this was a nine-year project in the making. Her ultimate goal was not only to win domestic titles but achieve continental glory and see her side crowned the best in Europe. We've seen enough to know that Chelsea are on the verge of something special, but just who is this mastermind behind the curtain?

2

Emma Hayes

PERHAPS IT is the longevity of her reign as Chelsea manager – given their rather quick turnovers in the industry – but Chelsea were looking for someone to build the team from the ground up as the start of a new project, and Emma Hayes seemed to be the answer. She has successfully kept the backing of club president Bruce Buck, director Marina Granovskaia, Chelsea Women chairman Adrian Jacob, and of course, the owner Roman Abramovich himself. The Russian oligarch wanted the women's team to become champions of Europe after finally tasting success from the men's side in 2012. They were formed during his second year as owner and he has gradually placed more importance on them over the years.

'[Chelsea Women] are a critical part of Chelsea and shapes who we are as a club. I see no reason why clubs wouldn't want to support women's football and provide the best possible opportunity for them to succeed,' Abramovich wrote in *Forbes*.

With his blessing, investments were made in this team – from improving the facilities to moving to Kingsmeadow Stadium. Just like he did with Andriy Shevchenko, Fernando Torres and Romelu Lukaku, Abramovich wants to sign the best players. The arrival of Pernille Harder commanded a world-record fee in the women's game while Sam Kerr has long been touted as one the best strikers around. Melanie Leupolz was a shrewd yet excellent signing from Bayern Munich. It's fair to say that Hayes was indeed backed with the tools to launch an assault at the UEFA Women's Champions League 2020/21 season and she almost succeeded by making their first final.

So what do we know about Hayes? The impression you get of the manager is one of someone full of passion, care and intellect. Having coached Chicago Red Stars and taking up a role as the assistant manager at Arsenal before landing the Chelsea job, Hayes has become a well-travelled individual who's developed herself across these adventures. These traits only describe parts of Hayes's overall personality, but each of those characteristics has emerged over the course of her time at Chelsea.

In *Forbes*, Abramovich continued, 'And I think investment pays off. I think their success demonstrates what can be achieved when you dedicate resources and the right leadership. Emma Hayes has been remarkable in her work with the team.'

These traits can be derived from her love for the job, paying attention to every meticulous detail from tactical nuances to player habits, and anything she can derive from other sports or paths. Almost every step of her life is an example that speaks volumes of her as a person and that seamlessly integrates into her management style. She joined Arsenal's academy aged 17 but then injured her ankle and was told she could never play again. Devastated, Hayes had to move on and find something else to do. She took up European studies, Spanish, and sociology at university with the intention of becoming a spy. Alongside her studies, she took up her coaching badges in football but also in other sports. She worked in sports development for the Camden council and even helped out in various family business ventures. She wants to succeed in everything she dips her toes into and that especially extended into her football.

Her endeavours didn't cure the itch and there was still a need for more. One day she chatted with her sister, Rebecca, and mentioned how she needed to be in an environment that was surrounded by high-calibre people in football to grow and learn from the best to improve her own skills as a coach and tactician. She ultimately made the decision to move to the United States with $1,000, a backpack, and a job at MLS Camps. The drive and dedication required to move continents with nothing but a punter's chance at success shows how determined she was to make it.

It was from there that her career as a coach really took off and she won a host of accolades, including the honour of being the youngest head coach in W-League history, as well as the Coach of the Year award in 2005. Her attention to detail in coaching and tactics is what sets her apart from her counterparts, displaying a high intellect and unique way of thinking. Her move to America propelled her to new heights because of the respect given to the women's game there at that time. Hayes had also made a real impression on the people there. She attended a United Soccer Coaches course in Brazil where Anson Dorrance, head coach at the University of North Carolina, who had led the United States Women to their first World Cup win in 1991, was in attendance. Given that he was an experienced practitioner of the game and had a vast wealth of knowledge, he was nonetheless blown away by Hayes's footballing intellect and her own knowledge. From then on, the two have kept in contact and whenever Dorrance visits England, he always meets Hayes at Cobham and learns from her training methods. It's these experiences that have contributed to her evolution as a manager and her period in America has enabled her to control people the right way through her intellect and passion.

'The thing that has always stood out to me about Emma Hayes is the person she is and how much she values the people she recruits. The emphasis she places on the personality of her signings is as great as the emphasis she will place on their quality and abilities. She recruits players who are good people and who value the team. Her players will always put the team first, even if that means they are on the bench or out of position. Her ability to connect with those players is second to none as well,' explained journalist Ameé Ruszkai.

However, what's most impressive is her man-management ability. You have the likes of Carlo Ancelotti and Thomas Tuchel who are renowned for their capabilities in managing their squad and keeping players happy. Hayes is of a similar mould, knowing just how to keep players on board and, most importantly, cared for. If you think about it, none of Chelsea's fringe players have ever come out publicly and complained about a lack of game time. There might have been talks internally, but not enough to be publicly disgruntled.

Hayes puts a huge emphasis on signing the right characters and she values personality above all else during recruitment. Two players might be of similar skill but only the one whose personality fits into the group will be recruited. Each player is almost hand-picked to join the squad, which shows the unity and cultured environment she's created. This is a testament to the way Hayes operates – making the whole squad feel included and acting like their 'mother figure'. Having experienced personal tragedy through the loss of one of her twins during her pregnancy in 2018, she knows what it's like to suffer real pain and devastating loss. So if there's anyone that knows how to deal with that, it's her and this means she knows what players need.

'Karen Carney told me a story earlier this year of her playing against Chelsea for Birmingham, and she got injured in the warm-up. Birmingham didn't have the resources Chelsea did and Hayes knocked on the changing room door, asked if she was okay and if she wanted to use Chelsea's physios and doctors. I thought that was poignant and really summed up Hayes and why her players adore her,' said Ruszkai.

Karen Carney is a player Hayes had once signed at Chicago Red Stars and then later brought to Chelsea. The midfielder became hugely successful with the Blues, going on to become a well-respected player in England. Both Hayes and Carney have grown close over the years, with Carney crediting the manager for being a monumental figure in her life. During Carney's stint in the United States, Hayes once secretly paid for her flights to the United Kingdom to see her sick mother. A bit-part player at the time, she didn't have enough money to fly back to England so Hayes funded everything. The visit back did her a world of good and made her happier upon her return, and it was only years later that Carney found out it was because of Hayes. Carney has also talked about her battles with depression that threatened to ruin her career, but even after Hayes was sacked as manager of Chicago Red Stars, she still worried about Carney's well-being.

'Emma's been incredible. She's been my rock; the person who made sure I was protected from everything. I had no idea what the illness was but she was the one questioning the doctor all the time,' explained Fran Kirby, speaking in *The Guardian*.

More recently, Kirby's return from injury is probably one of the best comeback stories of the decade. She had been plagued by a disease called pericarditis – an inflammation of the fibrous sac that surrounds the heart, known as the pericardium. It is known to make a person devoid of energy with symptoms including sudden sharp chest pains, fever, weakness, shortness of breath, and nausea. She credits Hayes for being her 'rock' and pulling her through the tough time she had during her injury.

We've seen Kirby go from being bedridden with this injury to a Ballon d'Or favourite in the space of 18 months. Her partnership with Sam Kerr has been phenomenal with her personal form being almost superhuman, but if it weren't for Hayes's willingness to keep her head held high, then we might have seen a huge potential tragically wasted. Kirby had thoughts of retiring during her illness but it was Hayes and her team-mates who convinced her to reconsider.

'There is no greater example of Hayes's player-management skills than her relationship with Fran Kirby. She has protected Kirby through her injuries, through her illness, through everything,' said Ruszkai.

* * *

When it comes to analytics and tactics, Hayes is not one who leaves anything to chance. Every game is checked and scouted with meticulous detail and then strategised, whether it be Brighton & Hove Albion or Barcelona. You need only hear of the story of journalists Suzy Wrack, Liam Twomey and Katie Whyatt sitting in Hayes's office for an interview where she spent an hour passionately discussing how Lyon could be beaten. Using a whiteboard with counters, she explained in full detail why they were the best team in the world and where they could hurt you. In typical Hayes fashion, she offered solutions and was raring to become the manager that beat the unbeatable. Though it was Paris Saint-Germain who ultimately bested their rivals in the 2020/21 Champions League, Hayes would still relish a chance to face Lyon; but her eyes will now be solely set on Barcelona.

They battled through arduous opponents in Atlético Madrid, Wolfsburg and Bayern Munich en route to that final, but it wasn't without its difficulties. In each instance, Hayes was able to adjust after the first 90 minutes and win the tie across two legs despite each of those teams finding weak points to expose. The final proved too much in the end and they faltered 4-0 to Barcelona. The new task at hand will be to slay the Spanish giants and take the throne. Tactically, we've seen many changes throughout her long stint but it is probably now that she faces her biggest challenge in navigating her way through another European journey.

These feel-good stories typify what Hayes is all about. We know her as an excellent man-manager and tactician, but most importantly, she is a kind-hearted person – someone who goes the extra mile whether it be for a player or game. Her life over the last two decades has been a rollercoaster of emotions but on the pitch, she's finally found success and a home at Chelsea. She runs the women's club alongside the guidance and guile of Granovskaia and Jacob, and it's their combined efforts that have driven the club to superstardom. That UEFA Women's Champions League Final might have been a culmination of nine years of work, but it could very well be a major turning point for the club. They won't rest until they've captured the title, but even if they do, would they have the credentials and tools to become Europe's next powerhouse?

3

Build-up and Attacking Tactics

'Under Emma Hayes, Chelsea have made themselves an incredibly fluid and adaptive team. Capable of lining up in various formations, and changing shape on the fly, the Blues constantly find ways to be adventurous in possession and use their defensive organisation as well to further their ability in regards to chance creation.' – Carlon Carpenter

ARGUABLY CHELSEA'S most impressive and aesthetic part of the team is their attacking potential. They have been an impressive unit for the last two seasons but have really raised the bar this season, continuing from where they left off. After being crowned champions, you could have forgiven them if they continued in the same vein, but Emma Hayes adapted and changed her tactics to suit the additions to the squad she made. Time and time again, teams have become complacent after a title-winning campaign due to a lack of fresh faces. An example can be found from the men's side of the club when Antonio Conte's Premier League-winning side in 2016/17 followed up with a disappointing fifth-place finish.

The summer of 2020 saw an influx of world-class players, creating a playing squad equipped to take on the UEFA Women's Champions League and defend their Women's Super League crown. As a result, Hayes had assembled a star-studded forward line that included the likes of Sam Kerr, Bethany England, Pernille Harder and Fran Kirby to complement Ji So-yun, Sophie Ingle and Melanie Leupolz in the midfield. What's even more impressive is how she's been able to mould this team into a well-oiled machine through not just her tactical acumen, but her impressive man-management skills as well.

The system only has room for a certain number of players so naturally someone is going to miss out, but you didn't really hear any rumblings of discontent coming out of the Chelsea camp during their title-winning campaign in 2020/21. So how does the team function going forward? This chapter will break down the attacking structure to truly understand the nuances in their tactics before diving into more in-depth detail of each concept.

When we look at Chelsea's tactical structure, it's important to understand the different areas that create a coherent and otherwise collective structure. They've mostly followed a similar system over the last few years with a few tweaks depending on the personnel available to them. There's been a relative evolution between 2017 and 2021 where different players have been the focal points of the system from which Hayes has built her team. We've seen Karen Carney, Ji So-yun, Fran Kirby, Bethany England and Pernille Harder all thrive under various systems and formations to get the best out of them. The ultimate aim is to create a united structure that can get the best of the squad to win the UEFA Women's Champions League. The tactics can be split into three distinct phases: build-up play, middle third transitions, and final third movement patterns. All three phases have their unique triggers and movements that integrate players from different areas to create a seamless flow of movement from one end of the pitch to the other.

Every player is connected with the final ball in some regard. Starting with the goalkeeper and central defenders, to the full-backs and strikers, each one has a part to play. There are three major parts to their attacking setup – the strikers, wide players and attacking midfielder (or number 10). Each of these players is part of a sequence that gels together to create their openings in the forward areas.

To better understand both their attacking and defensive mechanics, it's important to dissect their formation to better discern how it all comes together. The objective here is to give you an overview of how Chelsea play in the attacking and defensive thirds in their regularly used formations. Chelsea and Hayes have used a variety of formations in a 3-4-3, 4-2-3-1, 4-4-2, 4-3-3, and 4-4-2 diamond most recently. The 4-4-2 and 4-4-2 diamond in the 2020/21 season was their preferred approach having used the former system in 34 per cent of games and the latter 14 per cent of the time. They even used a 4-2-3-1 but ultimately, regardless of the system, the style of play was similar. Hayes wanted the front three to thrive and have the rest of the team supply them.

Each player understands their roles perfectly, which is a non-negotiable criterion for Hayes, one that also goes into her recruitment. She will only bring in players who have a high tactical understanding, which makes the team that much more efficient and thus she can fully utilise the squad. She doesn't just shoehorn players into a set system; rather Hayes drills the role required into the player until they perfect it.

The system itself is very fluid and doesn't exactly have a set shape when it comes to attacking in the final third. Many a time we've seen the three forwards interchange positions and transition in the attacking third with ease, moving defenders out of position. Whether it's the 4-3-3, 4-2-3-1, 4-4-2, or 4-4-2 diamond, there are certain movement patterns that govern the way Chelsea attack and break down the opposition. You could start with Kerr as the central striker with Harder plus Kirby flanking and see the next three attacking moves with Harder as the striker and Kerr at left wing. You could call this systematic freedom in a sense because the players are told to express themselves in a controlled environment. It's a system that Hayes has built to integrate and implement her squad players with their strengths in mind.

This has also meant having players like Harder or Kerr, who came from different playing styles at Wolfsburg and

Chicago Red Stars respectively, adapt well. Initially, both players took some time to settle but have now shown their true selves. Kerr recovered from her initial struggles to have a resurgent comeback, scoring 34 goals in all competitions in the 2020/21 season – including 21 in the WSL to win the Golden Boot. Harder, however, was painted as a player who regressed by only scoring eight goals in 17 WSL games compared to her 27-goal haul in the Frauen-Bundesliga. Though if we look closely, there is an argument to be made that Harder has actually improved Chelsea's overall output.

Having said that, the players aren't perfect so there are times when it may not come off, but that is offset by the individual brilliance these players bring to the table. A mazy run from Kirby or a finessed shot by Harder can make the difference in key moments during games.

There are similarities between the 2020/21 system compared to 2019/20. Let's briefly look back at the build-up and attacking tactics used in 2019/20 to comprehend what Hayes has changed and how much of an effect it's had on the current way of playing.

The 2019/20 season was different in a lot of ways where Hayes had decided to make a tactical switch from the previous year. Moving away from the 4-2-3-1 in 2018 to a predominantly 4-4-2 in 2019 was a change made to suit the profile of players in the squad at the time. If we can take a further step back to 2018, Fran Kirby was tasked with leading the line during that time, often playing as the lone striker and starting 20 games out of 22 matches in that position. However, her skillset is more reminiscent of a playmaker rather than a goalscorer. She often drops deep to collect possession and looks to either dribble or find a penetrative pass.

As a result, these movements ultimately create space for the likes of England, Reiten and Ji. Though this isn't to say she isn't a good striker – quite the opposite. Kirby thrives in the position as she's proven in the past, but it needs the right system, whether that means playing in a two-striker system or with a more attacking number 10 behind her. Kirby's biggest strength is her ability to receive possession in tight areas, relieving pressure and creating

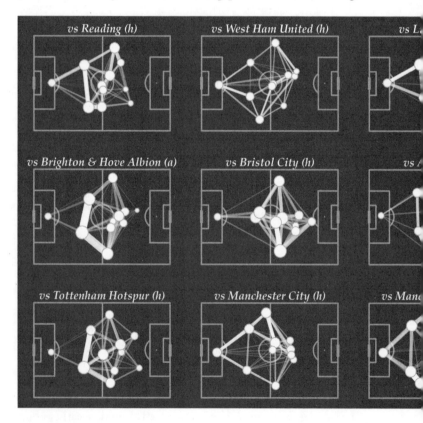

vs Reading (h)   vs West Ham United (h)   vs L

vs Brighton & Hove Albion (a)   vs Bristol City (h)   vs /

vs Tottenham Hotspur (h)   vs Manchester City (h)   vs Manc

space around her. But at the time, the problem was a mixture of very few midfield runners going beyond Kirby and the surplus of players of a similar profile operating in the same area.

The 2019/20 season saw a move away from the 4-2-3-1 formation with Chelsea then adopting a more native 4-4-2 system. The biggest, most obvious change was the switch to a two-striker system. This saw both England and Kirby start alongside each other in what was an excellent partnership. The two players' skillsets complement each

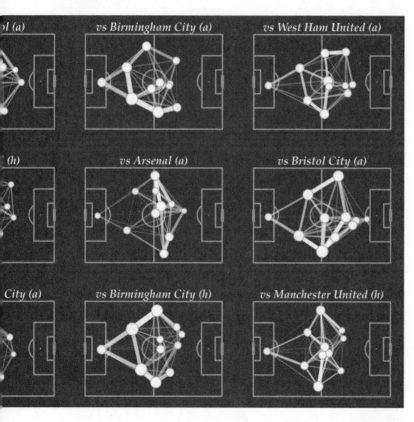

other very well in terms of their movement, positioning and space creation. This also saw Ji move to a deeper central midfield position alongside Sophie Ingle. *Figure 1* is an example of Chelsea's average positions and passing angles across the 2019/20 season, but what is most prevalent is how the central midfielders are always relatively close to each other regardless of the players pushing higher or deeper around them.

The two banks of four allow for better coverage and defensive solidarity along with more coordinated pressing from the front. Hayes liked her team to press from the front and in Bethany England, she has one of the best pressing forwards in the WSL. The front two would be two players who had differing profiles that suited each other's game.

The shadow striker allows teams to have a link player between the lines and carry the ball out wide to find the other striker. Kirby took up the shadow striker role, utilising her playmaking skillset to connect play between Ji and Ingle to England. The space vacated by Kirby opened up an opportunity for the wider players to drift in.

Most of the build-up play in 2019 was patient and careful with a mixture of playing out from the back and direct football. The make-up of the back four between then and now largely remains the same. Millie Bright, Magdalena Eriksson, Jonna Andersson and Maren Mjelde are all exceptionally talented players with the ball at their feet and are quite press-resistant. This means they're able to calmly play out of the press. The main strategy is to find the full-backs in a higher position. The central defenders would split wide and pass between each other if there are no clear and obvious passing options to either full-back.

This isn't to say Chelsea were not looking to progress through the middle – in fact, if the opportunity presented itself, then a central defensive midfielder would drop into the vacant space and pick up possession to push the play further forward. In Ji, they had an exceptionally creative playmaker who could not only pick a pass but also drive effortlessly with the ball and create goalscoring chances through the central areas, playing in the wingers or strikers. What we can see in *Figure 2* is the general setup and likely passing options for either centre-back and the spaces available if teams did press more aggressively.

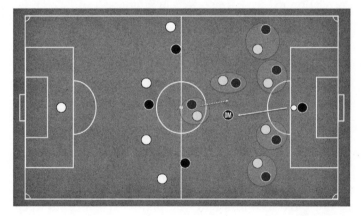

[Figure 2]

However, their main strategy was to go take a more direct route through long passes into the wingers which were often triggered by high-pressing teams. If teams commit players to the press, this opens space in behind for the wingers to engage in individual duels against the opposition full-backs. Ultimately, Hayes wanted her side to use the strength of her wide players by getting them on the ball and looking to play in the forwards, whether it be through crosses or going to the interior channels and playing line-breaking passes.

At the time, the numbers illustrated Kirby's improvement in her new position. Her number of passes has increased from 29.53 to 41.98 per 90 minutes and long passes from 0.65 to 1.91 per 90 minutes. This could be a result of the available space she has to roam and how she isn't restricted by being isolated as a lone centre-forward. Her dribbles have increased from 4.05 to 5.72 per 90 minutes which would have been in correlation to the space created by England and Ji.

Now that you have a better idea of the system she used in 2019/20, the later implementations can be better appreciated and understood to show Hayes's forward-planning measures. We know that she has predominantly used the 4-4-2 in 2019/20 and then became a lot more flexible to adjust to the opposition and personnel availability using a 4-3-3, 4-2-3-1, and later introduced the 4-4-2 diamond in 2020/21. This flexibility was needed to not only accommodate the players at hand but keep an element of unpredictability against tougher teams in both the Women's Super League and the UEFA Women's Champions League. Chelsea have a large squad and managing this group was a high priority.

The arrival of Harder also played a hand in forcing Hayes to rethink her tactics and come up with a more defined system to field all her attacking talent. There is a more developed and detailed chapter on the number 10 role and Harder's effect in relation to this role to come, so we can leave this for now.

Chelsea's build-up approach in 2020/21 was not too dissimilar to the way they played in 2019. They continued in their philosophy of patient approach play from the back and moving their way into midfield, where one of the central midfielders would find spaces to attack and pass forward. There is an emphasis on playing fast, agile transition football with the ball moving from defence to attack in the fewest number of passes possible. The end result is to have players in the box to receive a cross or pull-back and create an over-run. This is mirrored by Chelsea having the second-highest number of touches in the middle (335.4 per 90 minutes) and attacking thirds (217.9/90), just behind Manchester City.

The central defenders will again be patient in the build-up and find the right opportunity to find a forward pass, whether it be the full-backs or central midfielders. One of the main differences in the build-up strategy in 2020/21 was the use of rotations. Against low-block teams, Chelsea will continue to progress the ball through short passes into midfield, probing their way through. The idea was to pass it centrally, move it out wide, before finding a way back inside. Of course, against more high-pressing and better quality teams, Chelsea would seek a more direct approach with the centre-backs/central midfielder finding long diagonal or straight passes into the channels to bypass the opposition press. In *Figure 3,* you can see the difference in passing styles between Ji and Ingle where one is more expansive in her range of passing while the other plays more recyclable passes, keeping possession ticking over.

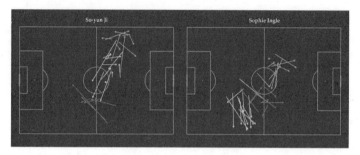

[Figure 3]

Chelsea will switch between a two- or three-player midfield depending on the formation which introduces Sophie Ingle into the mix, who will more often than not play as the deepest-lying midfielder. Her positional intelligence and calmness on the ball mean Chelsea have an assured presence during build-up; however, they mostly relied on a double-pivot, which will be expanded on later in the book.

Now, rotations have become important because constantly playing direct passes can result in a high turnover of possession which doesn't bring control. These rotations allow Chelsea to push more players up while keeping enough behind to secure themselves defensively. The central midfield pairing will aim to pull off into the spaces left by the full-backs who are encouraged to push up, especially when Niamh Charles started to play as a full-back. They don't become auxiliary full-backs but instead sit in the space between full-back and central midfield.

Leupolz or Ingle would drop in and become a temporary full-back which allowed the actual full-back to become a midfielder and contribute going forwards. This is where Chelsea were able to find an extra option in the wide areas and create a numerical advantage.

The addition of Leupolz facilitates these rotations very well because of her ability to be an excellent box-to-box midfielder and her positional sense from an attacking and defensive perspective. *Figure 4* highlights this concept and further indicates where Chelsea can have an advantage. There are several examples of this, some of which took place against Bayern Munich and Wolfsburg.

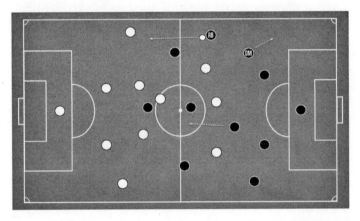

[Figure 4]

Not only does Leupolz control Chelsea's positional play but she also allows Ji to play slightly further forward, and more importantly, this allows Chelsea to field a press-resistant player who is adept at recycling and starting attacks. The German playmaker provides a reliable foundation to start attacks and find solutions against any type of opposition, whether they sit off or press aggressively.

When the ball reaches midfield, which starts the second phase of play, it triggers other players to make movements including the attacking midfielder who makes a move towards the side the attack is being played through. Here, the centre-forward is tasked with finding space by taking advantage of the space created by the other players. *Figure 5* illustrates the general patterns of movement of the players involved in the second phase of play and how it allows the forward to move more freely. The striker's movement gives the right-winger two options: to pass through the vacant space to allow the overlapping full-back and striker to receive or make a run inside using the space made by the striker's run.

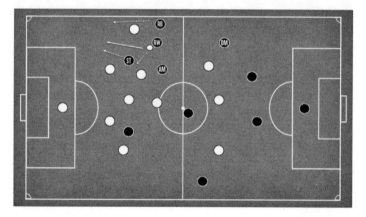

[Figure 5]

It is here where Chelsea want to control possession and dictate the pace of the game. The two midfielders are usually calm on the ball and will rotate possession until an opening presents itself in the wide areas. At their peak, they will connect the defence and attack without giving up on their positions. One midfielder is a deep-lying playmaker with box-to-box running tendencies while the other is a roaming, attack-minded dribbler who pushes the team forward with progressive running.

There are shades and elements in this to the way Olympique Lyonnais Féminin progress and build up. A lot of what made them such a hard team to press high against was the movement of the central midfielders and full-backs who rotated in tandem to create space and numerical superiority. Lucy Bronze, Saki Kumagai and Amandine Henry were excellent at this and it seems that Chelsea have adopted their own version of this concept. It gave Bronze a much more effective method of switching play to the marauding left-back, rather than being pressured in the wide area. They may not have taken this from Lyon but one can argue that they've possibly learned from one of the best teams in the last decade and adapted.

Regardless, while the two (or three) midfield players have different on-the-ball qualities, the attacking midfielder is arguably the most important player in unlocking Chelsea's attacking trio. This player needs to have the qualities to both provide a creative presence for the centre-forward but also create space through their movements off the ball. The position isn't too dissimilar to the way Chelsea used their second striker in the 4-4-2, where the primary function is to create space through lateral movement and drop into midfield to link up with the central players in build-up.

This is where Harder comes to make a difference. Her movement and relationship with Kerr and Kirby have been vital in Chelsea's attacking forays. Both Kerr and Kirby occupy an initial position and have set instructions regardless of formation, with Harder given the free role to operate in tandem. Harder normally occupies the number 10 position in Chelsea's off-the-ball shape with Kerr and Kirby in front of and to the right of the Dane. Her task is simple: hold a position between the lines and find vacant pockets of space in and around the area to run on to through balls or passes to feet.

[Figure 6]

Chelsea scored 67 goals with an expected goals (xG) of 57.4, which is an outrageous return. This meant they averaged the highest shot-creation chances per 90 minutes which also led to the highest goal-creation actions per 90 minutes in the WSL in 2020/21. These statistics can be directly linked to their build-up routine and attacking structure through the thirds and having every part of the team involved. *Figure 6* is a heat map that gives you the starting locations of passes that led to shots in 2019/20. Chelsea used the central areas around zone 14 a lot more compared to other teams, with the lighter spots around the deep half-space a result of long balls or through passes. Knowing this, it's easier to understand why Chelsea are now focused on switching play from mainly central areas and half-spaces to using the wide areas as a gateway into the 18-yard box. They may not use it to cross, but it is a method to manoeuvre their way in rather than predictably through the half-space. It's a way of getting around deep block systems that are played by the majority of teams against Chelsea in the WSL.

Depending on the position of the ball, Harder will move across to that side to create a numerical advantage and overload the half-space. In doing so, she's able to become the 'spare man' so to speak and drift between defenders unnoticed. The attacking movements of the winger, full-back and striker create enough chaos amid the move to enable Harder to drive between players and move in behind the defensive line. *Figure 7* is taking an example from the Continental Cup semi-final against West Ham where the first goal emphasises Harder's role as the number 10.

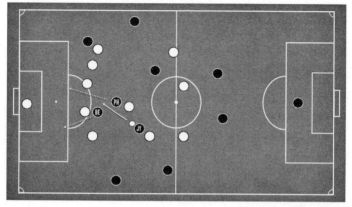

[Figure 7]

Ji makes a driving run from deep against a stacked, low-block West Ham defensive line with England and Harder just in front of her. There are three options here: either Ji passes to her left and plays in England; she drives forward herself and possibly wins a free kick; or she can play in Harder. She opts for the last option and what's interesting is how perfect Harder's timing is. Though there are three West Ham players in her vicinity, none of them pick up the Danish forward because she starts a bit deeper. Not to mention that Kirby is to her right, which makes matters for the Hammers players that much more complicated. *Figure 8* is a trend line of Chelsea's expected goals for (xG) and against (xGa) across every match week. The proficiency of the forwards is clear to see but what is more prominent was how generally cohesive the team was in attack and defence.

The idea for the forwards in this system is to be quick-thinking and move across the front line without being

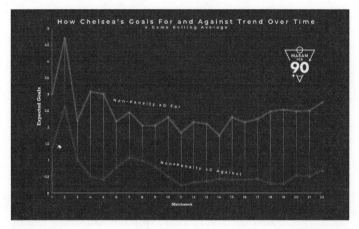

[Figure 8]

predictable while the midfielders have to play incisive passes in transition. The basic premise of the three players is to interchange positions through rotations and neat 'give-and-gos', pulling defenders out of position. This makes playing different formations much easier because the players aren't fixed in certain positions but rather being used as a reference point before becoming a fluid, amoeba-like front three.

Given the number of players moving around them both on and off the ball, the strikers need to evade their markers but also move into good goalscoring positions. The speed at which the midfield transitions means they have to always be on their toes. If a pass is played out wide and is crossed in by the right-winger, then the striker either needs to make a quick movement towards the ball to get away from a marker or use the same movement to allow a player behind her to get into a better goalscoring position.

What has been discussed here highlights and showcases how each and every part of Chelsea's team is involved from start to finish. Each player has their own set role and how they aim to make the system work. You can see how Hayes has crafted a well thought-out strategy to not only get the best out of her current squad but create an environment that encourages every player to play well. In theory, when you replace England with Kerr, you don't lose out on the core concept of the role, rather an enhancement due to the player's own qualities. Many of these concepts will be covered in more detail and depth in the following chapters, but the idea is to give you an overview of how this Chelsea side are set up to attack and build up.

4

Role of the Forwards

ARGUABLY THE 'Hollywood' glamour comes from Chelsea's forward line. In Sam Kerr and Fran Kirby, you have the 'Rolls-Royce' of forwards amid their ranks. Each of them is elegant, tenacious, and lethal in their own right, all from different backgrounds to come together and form a ferocious attacking unit. A bench with Bethany England, who was 2019/20's player of the season and second-highest goalscorer (14), Guro Reiten, and Erin Cuthbert only makes the attack more enticing.

While Kirby and England have been at Chelsea the longest, Kerr was one of the final pieces of the puzzle to form a trident that struck fear in the hearts of Europe's finest and now includes Pernille Harder. So, how does Emma Hayes integrate these players into her system? This is where we go into more detail on the role of the strikers to highlight the tactical nuances that bring it all together. Hayes's team setup is very system-specific rather than player-specific. Every player understands their role, which means that any change in personnel shouldn't change the overall performance. At the same time, the replacement players will bring some of their own qualities.

The performances of Kerr, Kirby and Harder have been excellent but the former two created an exquisite and unique partnership that blossomed towards the second half of the season. England has come in sparingly during the campaign but Hayes more often than not leant on the duo of Kerr and Kirby. There was a stretch of games between February 2021 and April 2021 where Kirby and Kerr would contribute to the other's goals and became affectionately known as 'Kerrby'.

The first goal against VfL Wolfsburg in the UEFA Women's Champions League quarter-final first leg displayed an almost telepathic understanding between the pair with Kirby playing a first-time pass through to Kerr. It should be noted, however, that the duo remained partly because of a head injury sustained to England which required a more cautious approach in making sure the player was 100 per cent healthy before returning to the pitch. This partnership would then be Chelsea's first-choice pairing and was integrated into Hayes's ideology in the final third.

Now, we know that the centre-forward has two essential functions in Chelsea's attacking setup. The first is their positioning which is based on the movement of other players around them that propels them to find as much space as possible. The second is that their movement becomes critical as they engage in deep link-up play, which means they need to be quick and accurate in their passing and have a good link-up ability. Additionally, they will drift into the half-spaces in the build-up to generate space on the shoulder of the defenders and make vertical movements.

This means the forwards have to be agile and use both diagonal and vertical movements to be able to get on to the end of attacking moves. The speed at which they transition and the way they move through the thirds means the strikers need to be aware of their position and know where the other forwards are. If a ball is played out wide and is crossed in by the winger, then the striker either needs to make a quick movement towards the ball to get away from a marker or use the same movement to allow a player behind her to get into a better goalscoring position.

The centre-forwards' movement, therefore, becomes important because they also create space for the other players, whether it be through vertical sprints or short diagonal runs to move a nearby player out of position. As mentioned in the previous chapter, the attacking midfielder plays a hugely influential role in creating the space for the centre-forwards to run into but is also tasked with sitting between the lines to pounce into vacant space and make ghost runs behind defensive lines. The centre-forwards' movement into the half-spaces moves defenders out of position, giving space for the number 10 to drive into the box and take up the striker's position which can be seen in *Figure 9*.

Here, you can expect a player like Kerr to drop into the half-space to overload with the full-back and central

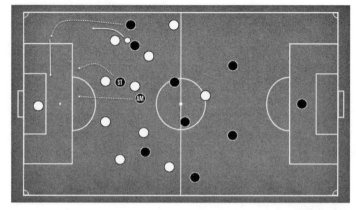

[Figure 9]

midfielder. The number 10 in the shape of Harder will provide some threat around this area but will ultimately move across to a more central position to spring on the spaces created by Kerr's original movement. Simultaneously, Kirby's position on the opposite side means players there are distracted.

When it comes to the relationship between the midfielders and strikers, there is a direct effect on Chelsea's efficiency in transition. A central midfielder will pick up the first ball out from the back and move it forward, and later become a more box-to-box player who will typically make late runs forward if there aren't enough players in the penalty area. Both deeper midfield players are interchangeable, especially when Ji So-yun and Melanie Leupolz play as the double-pivot given their attacking nature. *Figure 10* showcases these movements and how they can be effective especially against static, low-block defensive lines.

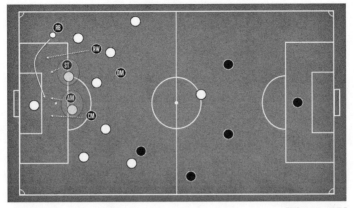

[Figure 10]

Chelsea want to move the ball quickly and in doing so, they opt for a more direct approach with the ball being played quickly all the way from the central defenders to the full-backs and central midfielders, then to where it finally ends up with the forwards. The idea is to get the ball into a dangerous area for the forwards to attack. However, what makes the double-pivot important is the central midfielders' ability to dictate Chelsea's point of attack. They choose to attack through the middle or wide areas, depending on the players available and opposition setup, resulting in quick and intricate passing exchanges. This invites the ball-side wide player, attacking midfielder, and striker to drop and engage in the attacking move to create numerical superiority.

The quick exchange will lead to a striker linking up play and becoming a playmaker of sorts by drifting into the half-space but ultimately will make a diagonal run behind to receive the final pass after contributing to the move.

Figure 11 is indicative of this where Kerr exchanged passes with Erin Cuthbert and Ji and raced through Manchester United's high line to create a one-on-one situation.

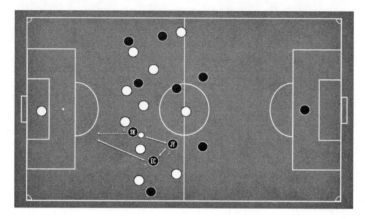

[Figure 11]

This is an example of how the movement of one deep-lying forward can exploit a team's defensive line. When Chelsea opt to build through the wide areas, which is the norm, they look to use the full-backs and have the ball-side players move across to create overloads and situations to break opposition lines. Ultimately, this allows more players to make late runs into the box and receive crosses.

Figure 12 begins a passage of play that illustrates Chelsea's movements going wide, starting with the second phase where Leupolz starts the initial move by dropping deep and passing it to Ji. She takes the ball forward and is faced by a wall of West Ham players but her thought is to move the ball out wide towards former Chelsea full-back Maria Thorisdóttir.

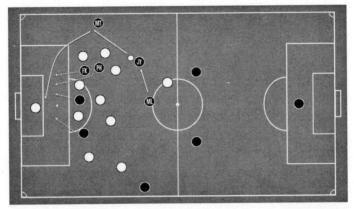

[Figure 12]

What is worth noting is how Harder's movement across from a central position to the near side next to Kirby creates an overload if Thorisdóttir were to come inside and pass it short. This sort of movement is critical from Chelsea's attacking midfielder, which will be examined in further detail in a later chapter. In reality, Thorisdóttir opted for the cross with Kerr, Harder, England and Kirby all in a position to make a quick and incisive forward movement for any pass that comes into the box.

This interchange of positions is the foundation of Hayes's attacking system because it allows Chelsea to break down stubborn defences while benefiting the three forward players. If Kerr moved out into the half-space to latch on to a deep pass, Kirby would then move into her position, receiving a deft, first-time pass. In effect, this would allow Harder to ghost through, sometimes unnoticed, and get on the end of a cross or pass. This had a profound effect on their scoring abilities and they were able to create and redefine how a strike partnership can work if paired correctly.

Defensively, the centre-forwards have an important function out of possession where they become the first line of defence that forms part of the overall defensive structure. The front three are responsible for starting Chelsea's press from the front in a systematic fashion. Hayes wants to give the opposition as little time as possible on the ball and force them into isolated areas to create a pressing trap and stop central passing channels. This is done through the forwards putting just enough pressure to compel the ball carrier to move in that direction. This section won't go into depth on the overall defensive structure and pressing right now; however, you'll get an idea of how the forwards are critical to Hayes's defensive strategy.

Kerr is a natural centre-forward while Kirby is a hybrid inside-forward/striker who plays in between the two positions. Harder can play as both a number 9 and 10, making her comfortable in both areas of the pitch. This changes Chelsea's shape and pressing tactic out of possession. They will almost play to the opposing team's setup and change their pressing shape based on that.

If the opposition plays with a dedicated number 6 as you would see in a 4-3-3, then Hayes has instructed Harder to play as a number 10 and cover, shadow and mark that player. This leaves Kirby and Kerr to pressure the centre-backs and block passing lanes to the middle. Kerr and Kirby will angle their runs to do this and just behind them will be Harder sweeping up in the next phase of play. In effect, this forces the ball out to the full-backs where they can be isolated or a mistake can be capitalised on. In this case, their goal is to stop the opposing team from playing through the middle and limiting the supply to the front three, which is illustrated in *Figure 13*.

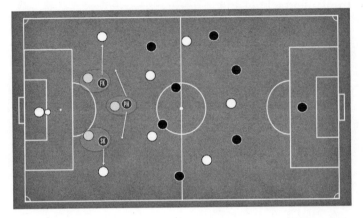

[Figure 13]

However, if the opposition uses a formation with a double-pivot or two sixes, then Chelsea's formation moves into more of a 4-4-2 diamond to press. The whole idea again is to create central compactness and limit the supply through the middle. This leaves the wide areas open, but Chelsea are happy to allow the ball to move down the wings and use numerical superiority in their low to mid block to regain possession.

From goal kicks, if the opposition decides to play it short, Chelsea have the numbers up front to press, but if they choose to go direct then there is more time for Chelsea to adjust their positions and bring their full-backs in or drop their midfielders back. As you read on, you'll begin to understand where and how these tactical nuances come together to create a complete tactical idea but it's astonishing to see the level of detail Hayes goes into, to create a situation that benefits the attributes of her forwards from an attacking and defending perspective.

5

Sam Kerr

*'Sam needed to move to Europe to take her
game to the next level.'* – Louise Taffa

STRIKERS ARE the main focus of any team, the ones
who hog the limelight with their goals and breathtaking
moments of glory. Two of the best male players of our
generation in Cristiano Ronaldo and Lionel Messi scored
40 to 50 goals a season for fun while the next generation
of Erling Haaland and Kylian Mbappé shows no signs
of slowing that trend down. All four of these players are
centre-forwards, each with a belief that they are the best.

Chelsea have historically been a club that have recruited
high-quality strikers across both the men's and women's
teams. From Didier Drogba, Eidur Gudjohnsen and
Nicolas Anelka to Eni Aluko and Bethany England,
these names have always been associated as focal points
of Chelsea teams. During the 2019/20 season, England
ended up as the second-highest scorer with 14 goals, just

two behind Arsenal legend Vivianne Miedema. The Blues didn't particularly need to recruit another centre-forward, but for a team with aspirations to win the UEFA Women's Champions League and progress as a squad, they needed to sign someone to compete with England.

Little did we know that Emma Hayes was plotting away to sign one of the best centre-forwards in football, with an excellent track record, be it in the United States or Australia. Sam Kerr was signed in the 2019 January transfer window and that made a statement of intent. It signalled Chelsea's desire to add to their star-studded squad with a focal point fitting to spearhead the team. Kerr's arrival was a significant coup, especially considering how they were competing with Olympique Lyonnais Féminin for her signature. The Australian rejected the chance to play with the then-European champions to instead move to England. It was a transfer long in the making for Hayes, with the Chelsea manager tracking her for almost three years before finally signing her for the Blues.

Fewer than five Australians have ever represented a Chelsea team with Kerr being arguably the biggest name of the lot. On the pitch, Kerr is a competitive, talented, mercurial centre-forward who dominates games for fun but off the pitch, you see a different side of her – one that almost surprises you given how talented she really is. Usually, the best players have a certain persona and ego about them but Kerr's pathway to football was unorthodox, to say the least.

Having started playing football at the age of 12, Kerr spent her time growing up playing Aussie Rules before moving into football. Just three years later, she became a full-blown international. In an interview with The Athletic, her mother, Roxanne Kerr, talked about her daughter without even mentioning that she was going to get her first international cap for the Matildas. Her first goal for the national side came at the age of 16 in the 2010 AFC Women's Asian Cup Final against North Korea.

After making her Matildas debut at the age of 15 in 2009, there was a feeling of euphoria around the young Aussie, but her transition to senior football wasn't the easiest. In 2011, Kerr had undergone surgery on her knee which meant she was out for an entire season at 18. Her return saw her find rhythm and flow but injuries were a regular theme throughout her early career. In 2015, she suffered a metatarsal injury and battled to make it for the Olympics. She shouldn't have been able to make the squad but she fought back against the odds.

When Kerr returned to full fitness and became injury-free, she would set out to become arguably the deadliest striker on the planet. Previously a winger, Kerr was moulded into a centre-forward because of her ability to isolate defenders and use her speed to take them on. Her coaches in Australia needed time to channel her focus into being more consistent, but the ability was there.

Kerr spent five seasons in the National Women's Soccer League (NWSL): three seasons with Sky Blue – now known as Gotham FC – and two with the Chicago Red Stars. It is arguably at the Red Stars that she made herself such an iconic goalscorer in the United States. She won the Golden

Boot in 2017, 2018 and 2019 along with a host of domestic individual awards, cementing her place in the record books.

By the time Kerr had turned 27 she had already competed at the 2011, 2015 and 2019 FIFA Women's World Cups as well as the 2012 and 2016 Summer Olympics. She has won the Women's Super League and Continental Cup; not to mention she's also played in a UEFA Women's Champions League Final. Her chapter at Chelsea did start off as less than perfect, however, with a struggle to put away chances in the beginning. People started to doubt her credentials and a rivalry was made between Kerr and Miedema for the title of the best striker in England, and possibly the world (though Ada Hegerberg may have something to say about that). But her first full season reminded everyone of her quality. This chapter will detail and give you a full understanding of how she's able to use her attributes to make her a top-quality centre-forward.

Kerr is an elite-level centre-forward who possesses a complete skillset that contributes to her overall level. Traditionally, she's been used as a pure goalscoring number 9 and while that is still the case, that has shifted slightly since her move to Chelsea. From her playing days at the Chicago Red Stars to Chelsea, there has been a change in approach by both managers and how they've decided to use her in their setups. In a nutshell, at the Red Stars, Kerr was a pure goalscorer with link-up play, while at the Blues there is a little more emphasis on interchangeability and link-up play, with more runners in and around her. There are similarities between her two stints but the system she played under makes the difference.

As is the case with other top players in this team, Kerr has come in and become an important component rather than the main focal point. In the USA, she was the player they built the team around, with every player contributing towards providing Kerr service. She responded by becoming a record-holder for goals and led the Red Stars to a championship final in 2019. They employed a 4-2-3-1 formation with the two supporting wide forwards playing in a narrower position. Katie Johnson and Yuki Nagasato aren't traditional wingers, thus they played close to Kerr.

However, Vanessa DiBernardo was arguably the most important player on the Red Stars' team. DiBernardo acted as the link player between the double pivot and strikers. With two defensive midfielders sitting behind her, DiBernardo was able to effectively thread balls towards Nagasato, Johnson and Kerr. Kerr particularly enjoyed playing with Nagasato to form a devastating partnership where the two shared a near-telepathic relationship. The game was centred around an almost counter-attacking style using DiBernardo and Nagasato's creativity to ensure Kerr got on the end of attacking runs off the last defender. Kerr would drop off to link up with the midfield but that was more to progress and provide a passing option. Her main responsibility and strengths were to find good attacking positions to create a pathway to get on to the goal. *Figure 14* shows a typical attacking pattern and Kerr's involvement.

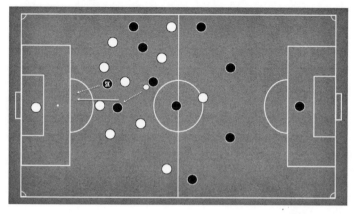

[Figure 14]

Looking back at an example from a game against Houston Dash, Kerr drops from between the centre-backs to pull them out of position with the ball being progressed to the number 10. From here, she makes a running start to go across the defenders and get into a one-on-one position against the goalkeeper. This one move showcases her intelligent movement, positioning and timing when it comes to getting into goalscoring positions.

At Chelsea, however, Kerr has developed her game and become a much more rounded centre-forward. From dropping into the channels to getting on the end of crosses, she is very aware of her surroundings and is a lethal finisher. Being the focal point of the attack, the Australian international is surrounded by a variety of player profiles which is one reason for her success in this position. Being able to interchange positions and being more involved in stringing together an attack, Kerr has become a better striker for it. Off the ball is where we see her strengths affect the team in a much-improved manner. Kerr always possessed excellent movement and timing which contributed to her high goal tally, but now she's using the same movement patterns to create space for the other forwards, making her combinations with Pernille Harder and Fran Kirby that much more lethal.

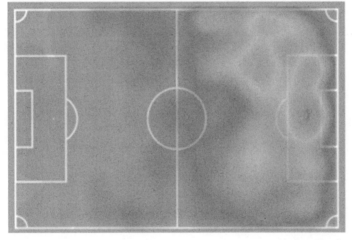

[Figure 15]

Kerr's heat map in *Figure 15* shows her favoured areas to operate in at Chelsea last season. This explains and highlights her movement patterns and gives us an indication of her playing style. What is most extensive is her activity on the left-hand side. Kerr tends to drift out into the wider areas, which almost makes it look like she's playing in a two-striker system as the left-sided player. To a degree, this is true because of the way Harder and Kirby operate and come inside, but Kerr's reasoning to do this is mainly down to her contributing to build-up and space creation. By moving into these spaces, she manages to move defenders around and attract markers away from their positions to open up space for the other forwards to move into.

You might have noticed that in some way, the three forwards are all tasked with a similar end goal but in their own given skillset. In Kerr's case, this is about space creation through movement and finding space in the box to finish off these moves. This is something she was exceptional at, as was evidenced by her 21 goals in the Women's Super League campaign.

More often than not, Kerr's starting position will be more central before she moves into the half-space or wide area to contribute towards the overload on that side. From here, the idea is to make sure the ball moves into a position to cross or pull back before she makes her way into the box to find a pocket of space. This can be both with and without the ball and given Kerr's agility in running,

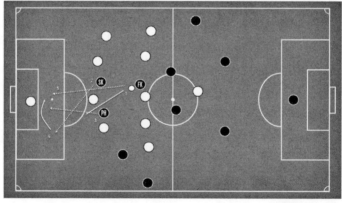

[Figure 16]

this makes it extremely difficult for players to track her movements. In *Figure 16* we have an example of this sort of movement from a game against Reading.

Chelsea are on the attack having broken through Reading's five-man midfield block, with Kirby receiving possession between the lines. Over here, the initial positioning of the players is important. Kerr starts in a central area while Harder is in the left half-space. Chelsea need to move the ball quickly before Reading can set up to defend any sort of through pass or cross to penetrate this back line. Kerr makes a diagonal move across, taking on Kirby's pass with Harder making an opposite run. The full-back marking Harder is then caught in between following Harder or re-routing to catch Kerr, which gives Kerr time to move across and open space for Harder to go through. The Reading defence was so focused on the other two that Kirby managed to find space in the centre of the 18-yard box where she receives a cut-back from Kerr to score.

This picture-perfect move was courtesy of a combination of all three players' movement, but it was Kerr's initial movement across the defender that ensured space was created for Harder to move into and later Kirby to get a free shot away. As far as the data goes, Kerr registered in the 96th percentile of progressive passes received per 90 minutes with 13.35, and in the 91st percentile for shot-creating actions per 90 minutes with 4.03 against all forwards in the Women's Super League. These numbers prove that she is a player who creates a high number of chances playing as the centre-forward because she's in a position to receive a similarly high number. This points to excellent positioning and decision-making.

Her movement has been critical in transition as well when Chelsea have exposed teams on the break. At speed, Kerr is one of the best players capable in one-on-one situations which gives her a reputation for being a world-class finisher. While we'll come to her finishing later in the chapter, her ability to move quickly to take advantage of the spaces is a feature of the Australian's game. For Kerr, it's all about her positioning which is the root of her successes as a centre-forward. Knowing where to stand to get to the right place at the right time is an incredible skill.

One part of Kerr's game that has been ever-present and arguably more utilised is her link-up play. A key part of Chelsea's attacking strategy is the link-up between Kerr, Kirby and Harder. The three of them are instrumental to the way Chelsea attack and create goalscoring actions. A forward like Kerr becomes a vital part of the interchangeability between the forwards because her movement is the initial trigger and dictates where the other players will move. If Kerr moves across then it gives Harder and Kirby their spaces to move into. The quicker the attacking move, the better they look. Kerr can operate both with her back to goal or in a counter-attacking situation.

Playing by holding off a centre-back or flicking the ball with a one-touch pass is a regular feature of the Australian striker's game. At times you'll see it work like clockwork with the three interchanging positions like a training ground drill. Emma Hayes has made the system so dynamic that it's given the forwards licence to roam and what's most impressive is the tactical nuances that have allowed each of the players to flourish in one aspect or another.

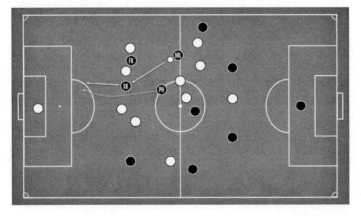

[Figure 17]

Let's look at *Figure 17*, where this passage of play is taken from last season's UEFA Women's Champions League Final against Barcelona. Though they were outclassed, there were still moments of brilliance from the forwards. Here, a move started with a quick pass from Melanie Leupolz into Kerr who drops to receive the pass. The two Barcelona central defenders, Mapi León and Patricia Guijarro, temporarily follow her which gives enough space for Harder to slip through. Kerr manages to play a one-touch back-heel pass between the defenders for the Danish midfielder to get on the end of. This sort of link-up is what makes Chelsea such a threatening force in the final third and given

Kerr's intricate feet, it makes the threat of the front three ever-present.

Kerr is in the 86th percentile of passes attempted per 90 minutes with 31.74 and has even attempted 2.49 progressive passes per 90 minutes. However, her standout statistic is her progressive carries, which lands her in the 80th percentile with 4.39. Therefore, we can conclude that Kerr is both efficient with her passing and with the ball at her feet; a player with an all-around skillset is a player that fits in well at Chelsea.

Arguably Kerr's greatest asset is her lethal finishing. Everywhere she's played, she has scored goals and ended up being among the top scorers. Kerr was the Women's Super League's highest scorer with 21 goals and won the Golden Boot, which made her the first player to win it in three different leagues. This Chelsea team has several high-quality players who are excellent finishers, but Kerr is undeniably the focal point for the side. Her goalscoring is the result of her excellent movement between the lines and positioning in the final third. Kerr knows which positions to take up depending on the type of attack being constructed. The tactical points mentioned earlier all show how Kerr can find space and end up in a position that puts her through on goal.

Kerr is sublime when it comes to one-on-one situations. Her ability to disguise her shot and find a corner away from the goalkeeper is one of her best traits. Take the example from Chelsea's UEFA Women's Champions League game against Benfica, where they transition quickly from defence to attack with Guro Reiten in possession. The winger, in a central position, sees Kerr on the edge of the defence on the right side. The Australian centre-forward makes a diagonal run across the full-back, takes one touch before slotting it down the goalkeeper's right.

The data is extremely supportive and backs the claim that Kerr is a fantastic goalscorer. She ranks in the 99th percentile for non-penalty goals (1.25), non-penalty xG (1.05), and non-penalty xG+A (1.33). Not to mention, she's in the 90th-plus percentile of shots total and assists. However, it's important to also see how many shots these goals have come from. Kerr took 86 shots with 39 on target. This equates to 5.10 shots per 90 minutes with a 45 per cent on target rate.

Twenty-one goals from 86 shots is a very high frequency and there is an element of wastefulness, but across a season it means she has an approximate 24 per cent conversion rate. Does Kerr need a high volume of shots to produce

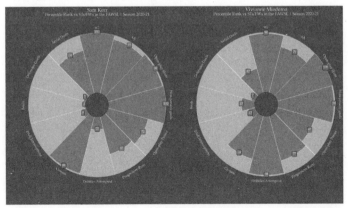

[Figure 18]

73

goals? Yes – but if given four or five chances a game, she surely puts at least one away.

When compared to Vivianne Miedema, Kerr does excel in some areas. *Figure 18* is a graphic that contains the statistics of both centre-forwards from the 2020/21 season. We can see that Kerr has more goals per 90 minutes and scores them with slightly fewer shots than the Dutch international. Even in shot-creating actions, Kerr outperforms her counterpart though she's played fewer full 90-minute games.

'For a player that's admitted to "hating" football as a kid, Sam Kerr is a natural gamer. She's got a nose for goal and, despite a slow start coming into a side full of stars, has made herself an essential part of Emma Hayes's plans. Plus, she has legendary victory celebrations — and what better place for Sam to lift trophies and party at the end of the season? She and Chelsea are a perfect match of ambition, joy, and winning ways,' said Dan Dormer.

As far as world-class strikers go, Kerr is up there as one of the best. She's on a level with little company alongside Ada Hegerberg, Miedema, Jenni Hermoso, and Marie-Antoinette Katoto as Europe's most elite centre-forwards. As the club continue to strive for excellence, Kerr will grow with them. She already typifies the profile of a player the club are looking to attract, and the arrivals of Harder and Leupolz follow that model. Granovskaia played an influential role in attracting the Australian, who had reported interest from Olympique Lyonnais Féminin, but in the end, Kerr was convinced by the project Hayes was trying to build. Was her choice vindicated? Possibly, as they did reach a Champions League Final, but the goal will now be to go all the way and become one of the faces of this long-standing project. Chelsea is a club that breeds success, and Kerr is a representation of that.

6

Fran Kirby

'Kirby was arguably the best player in the world last season, leveraging her tremendous technical qualities and explosiveness to bend and ultimately break defences as a needle player and threat off the shoulder.' – Om Arvind

IT COULD have all been so very different. Fran Kirby has seen much of life at such a young age given the traumatic nature of her teenage years. She has suffered heartbreak and setbacks throughout her career, and what you see now is a culmination of hard work and a determination to make it to the top. To truly conceive what Kirby has achieved in a footballing sense, we need to take a step back and appreciate the gruelling path towards greatness.

At age 14, Kirby felt something that no one should have to go through – the sudden loss of her mother. During that time, she was making her way in football and by 16, she was making her debut for Reading who were then in the second tier of English football. Three years from her mother's death, Kirby fell into a deep depression and quit football altogether just as she was beginning to demonstrate her raw talent.

Only her mother's wish of Kirby fulfilling her destiny to become a professional footballer brought her back into the fold, and having rejoined Reading, she helped propel them to Women's Super League 2 in 2014 with 24 goals in 16 appearances. These types of performances caught the eye of the bigger clubs and landed her a British record transfer to Chelsea. After a good start to life at Chelsea, the 2019/20 season sadly saw Kirby out of the starting 11 and eventually out of the matchday squad.

It was in November 2019 when she was diagnosed with pericarditis, a heart disease that would keep her out for nine months. The club only released a statement four months later once she felt better. In an interview with *Goal,* Kirby revealed that there were doubts about her return to the pitch.

She later told *The Guardian*, 'There was a period, where I was told by the cardiologist that if I don't slow down, I could become chronic and not play again.'

Kirby credits Emma Hayes in both her professional and personal development as one of the people who was heavily involved in her recovery. Hayes offered a comfort that only a mother can give, and that meant more to Kirby.

Coming back to even be named on the team sheet was an incredible feat, let alone producing match-winning displays week in, week out. Kirby's return was a huge boost for a side that already boasts the likes of Sam Kerr, Pernille Harder, and Magdalena Eriksson. However, the way she performed and contributed has been unlike anyone has ever seen, with her influence seen in almost every game she was involved in. Sixteen goals and 11 assists for a wide forward are the numbers you want from one of your main attacking threats.

Chelsea and Hayes's quest to become an elite-level club competing in the latter stages of the UEFA Women's Champions League and winning multiple domestic titles is under way, and the last two seasons have been proof. However, every successful team needs a well-balanced, yet elite-level squad to mesh and contribute to the cause. Kirby is one of the superstars of Chelsea's team with a profile and story that cultivates greatness.

'Kirby arrived at Chelsea with a massive billing: she was the most expensive female British player of all time, had just torn WSL 2 apart and Mark Sampson had called her England's "mini Messi" at the World Cup in 2015, where she was her country's only player outside of the top flight,' said Ameé Ruszkai.

The culmination of reaching a first UEFA Women's Champions League Final comes in the wake of Kirby's return, and while she was always integral to their success in previous campaigns, it is only now that she's shown her greatest return in form which has seen Chelsea reach this milestone. Her combination with Kerr and Harder has been superb to create Europe's most in-form and lethal front three. So, how does such a player perform in this system, and what aspects make her so important?

Kirby is a multi-faceted player capable of playing in multiple positions because of her versatility. She's traditionally been an attacking midfield playmaker occupying the number 10 position, but she's also played as a natural centre-forward in past seasons. Kirby has been the team's primary playmaker and link player, supplying service for strikers for both England and Chelsea. This past season, however, she's become much more involved as an attacking force coming in off the right wing. Chelsea have structured their system in such a way that allows Kirby to start in a certain position but is able to attack the channels like an inside-forward as well as make bursting runs in behind the defence like a box-to-box midfielder.

From a holistic perspective, Kirby's strengths are based on her intelligence, movement and vision, which shines through her passing, ball progression and finishing. It's important to look at where she's played in this time and, as mentioned, her influence has mainly originated from the centre-forward or attacking midfield position. To put this into context, in the 2018/19 season, she was used as a striker in 82 per cent of the games she played (22). In 2020/21 she was used primarily as a right-sided attacker but was frequently moved across the front line. The fluidity of the current system meant she didn't have a fixed position; rather her role transferred across the positions, carrying out similar tasks.

Timing and identifying space in the box are critical in her role and are a major part of her high goalscoring exploits last season. Her movement into the box coupled with her telepathic connections with Pernille Harder and Sam Kerr meant she usually found space and was at the right place at the right time in almost every instance. In *Figure 19* you have Kirby's heat maps from both the 2019/20 and 2020/21 seasons to give you a comparison of her movement patterns and areas of activity. There is a distinct change in the areas of occupation going from a primary forward to effectively a right-sided player but more importantly, one that starts wide and moves in towards the right half-space and inside the box. Hayes wanted Kirby more involved and her partnership with Kerr was something she anticipated when signing the Australian, which is a point that will be elaborated on later in the chapter.

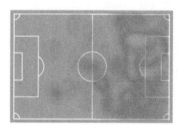 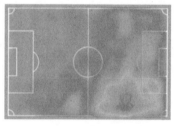

[Figure 19]

So these movement patterns are the core competency that makes up her strengths, which helps the team to break down opposing defences that employ both low-block systems and high lines. There are two phases to Kirby's game that include her movement – one when the build-up is on the left and the other on her side. When Chelsea build up through the left, it means Kirby is tasked with taking advantage and finding space in one-on-one situations to get in behind the opposition full-back. This creates openings by the opposition being dragged out of position which result in an underload on her side. This underload creates a situation where Kirby has one player to get past, and because of her superior dribbling and ball carrying, she's able to beat most full-backs. *Figure 20* is an illustration that showcases this type of movement, including her starting position and the pathway she takes to get into a goalscoring position. She'll start wide on the right and make a curved run around the defender to get in behind the full-back and make a darting run across the box to get on the end of any pull-backs or crosses.

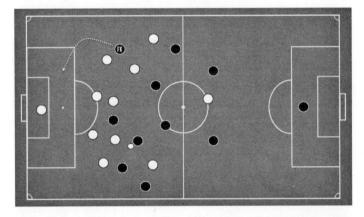

[Figure 20]

A lot of Kirby's goals have come through this route and her sense of positioning and timing plays a big role in how she's able to do so. In the past, she's always been a central figure when it came to playmaking and attacking, taking on a centrally focused role whereas now, Kirby has adopted a slightly 'freer' role that enables her to play between the lines more and make decisions based on what is going on around her. Between 2017 and 2019, Kirby scored a combined total of 23 goals and six assists, but last season she registered 16 goals and 11 assists. On the surface, it's her positional change that has enabled her to get into better goal-creation and scoring positions, but the change in position has enhanced her excellent vision, movement in space, and timing. *Figure 21* is a pass network from Chelsea's game against Wolfsburg and Kirby's positioning in the wide right here is an indication of her freer role where she's able to create and make more unmarked runs from the back post.

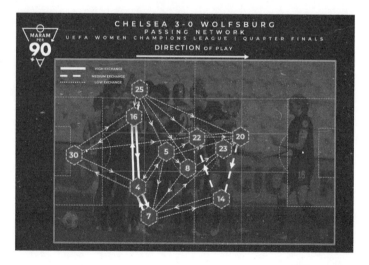

[Figure 21]

When it comes to ball progression, Kirby is an excellent ball carrier and the ball seems to be glued to her feet. A maestro in possession, she's able to use her exceptional dribbling ability to get into positions to create a shot-creating action or a key passing opportunity. Her positioning and smart movement between the lines allows her the space and time to get into these types of positions. The movements by Harder and Kerr allow her to utilise the vacant spaces to drive forward in the final third. With Chelsea being such a dangerous transition team, Kirby can use her dribbling to take on players and become the magnet to attract defenders towards her. This, in turn, gives space to Harder and Kerr to get into goalscoring positions.

Sounds familiar, doesn't it? It's because at some point, the basic principles of the forwards' roles are the same: create space through effective movement patterns between the lines, causing defensive lapses in concentration. This sort of breakdown of defences is what allowed Chelsea to score a plethora of goals throughout the season. Only teams who could nullify the front three's movements, or at least block two of them, were successful, but even then they were affected by midfield runners. Barcelona were one of the few teams who successfully thwarted the front three's effectiveness while Bayern Munich and Wolfsburg only did it in bursts. The next two examples will highlight instances of Kirby's strengths in creating chances and scoring with her dribbling.

Figure 22 takes a passage of play from a game against Atlético Madrid Women in the UEFA Women's Champions League, where Kirby picks up possession in a deeper position on the right and drives forward through

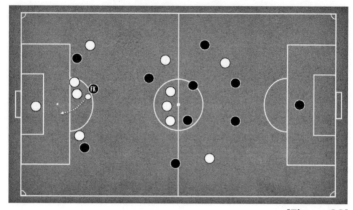

[Figure 22]

a sea of players. When she reaches the edge of the box, Kirby manages to drag two defenders towards her and makes a quick dash to her left and gets a shot away. When she drives with the ball, she's able to keep possession and dance past defenders with ease. We'll see more of this in the next section, but her ability to interchange passes with players around her is as good as anyone else in the league.

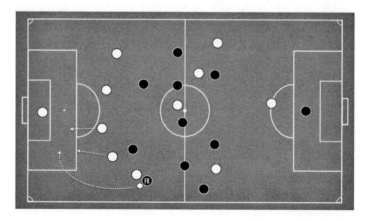

[Figure 23]

This next example is taken from a Women's Super League game against Manchester United where she picks up possession at left wing and is up against defensive midfielder Hayley Ladd as is seen in *Figure 23*. The midfielder should be able to shepherd Kirby into the corner, but the English forward uses her burst of speed to drive past her into the vacant space behind. Once she reaches the box, she's faced up against the centre-back but from here, she stands up to the defender and passes across to the centre for Kerr.

In both scenarios, Kirby has shown a propensity to go from deeper, less favourable positions into a place where she can create a goalscoring or chance-creation action.

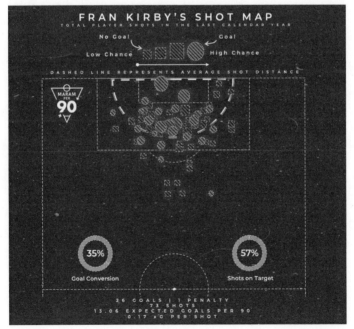

[Figure 24]

This season has been Kirby's best to date, both in terms of how she's playing on the pitch and the numbers she's producing. *Figure 24* is Kirby's shot map and implies where her shots are taken from and the quality of chance. With most of her high scoring chances in the 18-yard box, it shows how effective she is at finding space in the box.

The data supports her here, with Kirby ranking in the 98th percentile for shot-creating actions with 6.01, and ranking in the 93rd percentile for progressive carries with 7.05, both against all of the attacking midfielders and wingers in the Women's Super League. Both metrics are a way of measuring how influential she is with the ball for Chelsea and the way they want to play in the final third. Kirby's role as a creator has been evident because of her playmaking and while she's added more goals to her game, her assist numbers have gone up too. Ignoring the 2019/20 season, Kirby's assists per 90 minutes has been at an all-time high during her time at Chelsea. Averaging 0.72 per 90, Kirby has shown how she's been able to incorporate her goalscoring exploits along with improving her playmaking.

Kirby's playmaking comes through her incredible vision and creativity that is shown through her exquisite passing abilities. When she enters the final third, Kirby thinks objectively and manages to make correct decisions quickly at the moment. If the move calls for a pass, then she'll make that move; otherwise she'll dribble and find a shooting opportunity. Her passing range includes a whole host of approaches such as crosses, through balls, diagonal passes, and key passes. She has a repertoire to carry out any type of pass in any given situation. Given her press-resistant style of play, Kirby can churn out a smart pass in the tightest of situations.

These actions have been a critical part of the way the front three work together and combine. Though Harder and Kerr are decent passers of the ball, they lack the technicality and finesse of Kirby. She's able to find her team-mates with extreme precision even in pressure situations. Whether she's positioned on the right or centrally, her passes often find their intended target. This is reflected in her pass completion rate of 77.4 per cent, putting her in the top performers of this metric in the league.

Her best passes are the ones where you think there are no options available, yet Kirby is still able to play an inch-perfect pass threaded through a crowd of bodies. Throughout the season, we saw Kirby make some incredible through passes that have split open defences. Let's take this

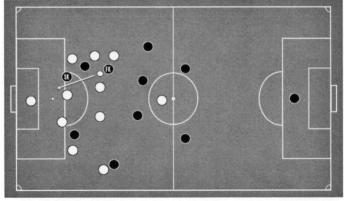

[Figure 25]

example in *Figure 25*, where Kirby shows incredible vision and skill against Bristol City.

Here, Kirby picks up a short pass from Hannah Blundell, where she immediately turns and spots a gap between Bristol's defensive line where Kerr makes a sprint to beat the last defender. Kirby sees Kerr's run and manages to thread an acute line-breaking pass to play in the Australian, putting her in a one-on-one position against the goalkeeper. Another example that comes to mind is a moment where Kirby was faced against a low-block Reading defence, and after a quickfire exchange of passes, she managed to play a chipped ball into the path of Kerr that nullified the defence almost instantaneously. The vision to receive, turn, scan, and make the pass in the space of five seconds sums up Kirby's game judgement. Very few players have the intelligence and talent of the Lionesses forward, and the relationship between her and Kerr is a testament to that.

The two players were inseparable last season given that a majority of Chelsea's goals were courtesy of the Kirby–Kerr partnership. The pair have scored a combined 37 goals with 18 assists in the 2020/21 season, making them one of the most prolific partnerships in Women's Super League history. Together they have been involved in more goals than anybody else in the league and set a new WSL record in setting each other up for 12 league goals. This sort of partnership requires chemistry, understanding, and trust to know that the player will be at the right place at the right time. While the three forwards have combined well in general, which was seen in the aforementioned chapter and the discussion on positional rotations, the intelligence to find each other is one that only a few striking partnerships can muster. Harry Kane and Son Heung-min is a recent example of a better record with 14, but it's a testament to the Chelsea duo in how they've adapted considering this was Kerr's first full season in London.

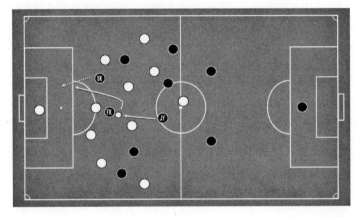

[Figure 26]

This goal contribution is probably a standout moment from Chelsea's run in the UEFA Women's Champions League during their home leg against Wolfsburg. At 0-0, the game was in the balance when Wolfsburg should arguably have been one to two goals ahead. Kirby's one moment of brilliance flipped the game on its head and put the Blues 1-0 up. In *Figure 26*, you can see Kirby's initial position where she receives a pass from Ji So-yun in between the lines, and almost instantaneously turns and plays a pass through Wolfsburg's defence. She anticipated the move from Dominque Janssen to come across slightly and mark her, so instead of holding on to the ball, she releases it for Kerr to make a central run through the middle. The Australian centre-forward takes the ball away from the Polish goalkeeper Katarzyna Kiedrzynek and breaks the deadlock. The movement and skill to finish the move were sublime by Kerr, but it was the vision and intelligence from Kirby that makes it an opportunity worth pursuing. This example showed the high skill level that's innate in both players where they can take seemingly improbable situations and turn them into a goalscoring or shot-creating action.

Kirby's story has been nothing short of phenomenal and the road to redemption has been simply exemplary. The comeback from her hellish injury to become Chelsea's and Europe's standout player this season is one that will live long in the memory of all fans. Being so versatile, Kirby has transcended into a truly elite-level player now, recognised by the world. When you talk about Ada Hegerberg, Vivianne Miedema and Pernille Harder, you also include Fran Kirby in that list. Replicating the Europe-conquering squads of Olympique Lyonnais and Barcelona is what Chelsea strive to do, and having a player of Kirby's calibre is a necessity.

Having a prime Kirby means Chelsea need to capitalise on her excellent form now with all the pieces of the puzzle in place. Kirby completes the trident and has become synonymous with Chelsea's core success. You can argue that Kerr and Harder could be dropped from the starting line-up, but Kirby is the glue that keeps the attack together and can operate without them. She's integral to any tactical changes Chelsea and Hayes may opt for in the 2021/22 season. Given that she's now able to consistently contribute both goals and assists, she now becomes the player Hayes builds around. There is no reason for her not to go on and become Chelsea's greatest-ever player, and be a part of their quest to become Europe's next powerhouse.

7

Chelsea's Number 10 Role

EACH COACH has their variation of the role and position, and Chelsea are no different. Emma Hayes has operated with and without the position in her side, going from a 4-2-3-1 to a 4-4-2 in the last few seasons. Now she's turned the system into a very flexible formation which also sees her go back to using an attacking midfield position. Hayes wants a player in and around the front two strikers to help facilitate their movement in either of her formations. In the past, she's used Ji So-yun as an advanced, ball-carrying playmaker who was a key part of Chelsea's attack. This time around it's slightly different because of both the structure and the players around her. To describe what the position entails is relatively simple, but in nature is much more detailed. Chelsea's use of the position is designed to incorporate a player who is willing to be a workhorse and in some sense sacrifice their output for the betterment of the team.

The position's job description includes two major responsibilities that need to be carried out, with anything extra brought by the player as an added luxury. Positional intelligence and awareness combined with the out-of-possession movement encourage high chance creation. The position isn't so much about what the player can do on the ball but rather what they can do off it.

The attacking midfielder is both the link and reference point in the final third given that any moves will run through this player in almost every attack. In the first phase, they aren't primarily expected to create goal-contributing actions but rather connect play and find space. Let's expand on this point. When Hayes brought this position back upon signing Pernille Harder, the intention wasn't to only put the Dane in a position of comfort but to also unshackle Fran Kirby and Sam Kerr. The role is inherently made to facilitate the two centre-forwards while also opening space for the full-backs to affect the game. This starts with the continuation of the build-up in the final third. Here, the number 10's responsibility is to ensure that the ball is received and released quickly into the channels for the mobile striker or full-back to collect and move on to the second phase of attacking play. The role was meant to be one that facilitated and allowed the front two players to wreak havoc by putting them in favourable positions, which is illustrated in *Figure 27.*

When the ball is played forward into the number 10, the player drops slightly deeper to collect but in doing so, will attract the attention of the neighbouring central defender and/or number 6 which already starts to break the opposition's shape. A pass into the channels or wide

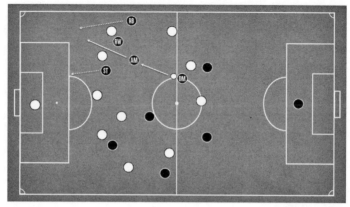

[Figure 27]

area forces the opposition to shift across and focus their attention on the full-back, striker, and attacking midfielder, creating a three v two scenario. In this case, you see how the player affects the movement of both her team and the opposition team which unsettles the players and unless there's discipline in moving back into position, it starts to create small cracks.

We know that Chelsea use their full-backs to support attacks by being part of the overloads, but the number 10 will move across and influence the timing of said attacks. This player will choose both the timing and type of pass for the best possible outcome. From here, the ball will make its way from the channels to a central cross or pull-back.

Just before this, the attacking midfielder will drift away and exploit the defenders that are ball-watching, and then time her run to ghost through the defence to get on the end of the aforementioned cross.

Simultaneously, there is an element of underloading on the opposite flank where the other winger will be left in a one-on-one duel against the full-back. So while the movement across the channel creates space for the centre-forwards and subsequently the other winger/forward, the following movement is important because this is where the attacking midfielder uses the same sort of movement to find spaces to get into goalscoring positions. Their task is to position themselves in between the lines to not be easily marked by opposition defensive midfielders. This positioning intelligence means the centre-back and defensive midfielder have to be seamless in marking this player. If we continue using the previous example in *Figure 28*, you can see the path the attacking midfielder chooses to move into to find space between the lines and ultimately set themselves up for an attacking run into the middle.

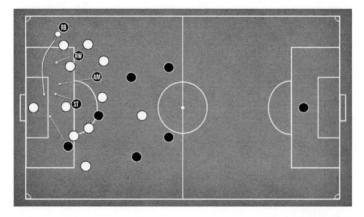

[Figure 28]

If this is how the number 10 position is used at Chelsea, then how does Harder fit it? Before we can go into the deep-rooted tactics that involve the Danish international, knowing who Harder is away from the football pitch and the factors that have made her one of the world's best players will give us a real insight into how that translates to her on-field performances.

Erin Cuthbert celebrates after scoring her side's first goal in the FA WSL match between Chelsea Women and Birmingham City Women

Magdalena Eriksson – Chelsea's rock and captain.

Marina Granovskaia presents Melanie Leupolz signing from Bayern Munich in March 2020.

Pernille Harder celebrates with Bethany England.

Chelsea celebrate together as Hannah Blundell scores her side's second goal during their game against Everton Women.

Chelsea lift the Barclays FA Women's Super League Trophy as they are crowned champions once again.

The moment Emma Hayes' side won the second leg of the UEFA Women's Champions League semi-final match against Bayern Munich

Jessie Fleming celebrates her first Chelsea goal against Manchester United

Emma Hayes celebrates by lifting the Continental Tyres League Cup Trophy.

Fran Kirby wheels away in celebration after scoring the first goal during the second leg of the UEFA Women's Champions League semi-final match between Chelsea and Bayern Munich.

8

Pernille Harder: The Modern Number 10?

'She's like a magician that leaves you speechless
after she puts on show after show. Her
movement with the ball is like no other, no
angle is too tight, no distance too far – she
always finds a way. And if it's not her, she
has the eye for someone else. She's the complete
package and everything you want in a player.'
– Jasmina Schweimler

PERNILLE HARDER was destined to be a footballer, it seems. Growing up in a footballing household, there was very little else she was exposed to. It is little wonder that it would be the world she would be thrust into given that both her parents and sister played, making Harder's inclusion inevitable. The Dane was born and raised in the little-known town of Ikast with her father being a Manchester United fan. Memories of David Beckham,

Ryan Giggs, and of course, the great Dane himself, Peter Schmeichel. As is customary for her generation of players, Harder started her footballing journey playing with the boys' team at FC Midtjylland until the age of ten, though she initially started with a young girls' team. She knew from an early age that there was something special about her. A talented individual, Harder predicted her pathway to becoming a professional footballer by primarily plying her trade in the Frauen-Bundesliga and for Denmark.

Her stock rose as she developed her skillset and eventually made her way to the Danish top-flight side IK Skovbakken. Twenty-two goals in 27 matches grabbed the attention of Scandanavia's finest but an even more remarkable achievement was being called up to the senior national team at the age of 16, only a year after playing under-17s football. A hat-trick on her debut in a 15-0 win over Georgia announced her on the world stage. Three years later, she made the move to the neighbouring Linköping to stop the domination of Tyresö FF and Rosengård. In four years, Harder helped lead Linköping to a league title.

Aged 24, a dream move to Wolfsburg presented itself after a Damallsvenskan title and 24 international appearances. Her first 18 months in Germany was almost the perfect start, the highlights being two domestic doubles and playing in a UEFA Women's Champions League Final. Harder moved to Wolfsburg to play in the biggest games against the best teams, and Olympique Lyonnais Féminin were the ones to beat. She almost led them to that win single-handedly, but an Alexandra Popp red card swayed the tie in Lyon's favour and they lost 4-1.

She's had a fledgling international career where she reached the final of the UEFA Women's European Championship in 2017, losing out to the Netherlands. Though she's had domestic success, it seems that Harder isn't able to get over the line in finals, be it continental or international. This continued in the 2019/20 season when Wolfsburg reached yet another final and faced their arch-nemesis, Lyon, again. The first 45 minutes gave Wolfsburg a glimmer of hope but the French Queens of Europe produced one final performance to win their fifth straight UEFA Women's Champions League title. The Wolves were crushed, with Harder faltering at the final hurdle once again. Enter Emma Hayes and Chelsea. The Blues were quick to act by making the Danish midfielder the world-record signing they needed to complete their attacking trident.

Her first season in English football has been a relative success. A league and cup double have constituted instant success for the Dane, but yet again after making another UEFA Women's Champions League Final, Harder was unable to taste victory after a humbling 4-0 defeat to Barcelona Femení.

However, Harder's story doesn't end here. At 28 years of age, she's in the prime of her career and can lead Chelsea's quest to European glory. Alongside Sam Kerr and Fran Kirby, Harder has formed a formidable partnership and understanding. The rest of this chapter is dedicated to providing a full, comprehensive understanding of

Harder the footballer and what makes her arguably the world's best.

The number 10 position has been used in a variety of systems and roles with each iteration evolving into a more refined version of its original form. The modern version of this role no longer has a number 10 that we're used to seeing with a traditional playmaker – rather it has become a position that requires a lot more discipline, work rate, and attacking endeavour.

Dzsenifer Marozsán, Debinha, Rose Lavelle, and Daniëlle van de Donk are four examples of different number 10s, each with their style of play and system they work under. Marozsán is a tactically and positionally intelligent player with acute passing abilities to break down defences and assist in goals. While Lavelle and Debinha are very direct attacking midfielders whose games revolve around their ball-carrying and goalscoring abilities, van de Donk can be described as a player with rugged tenacity and an elegant passing technique that suits a tiki-taka style of football.

Indeed, Arsenal have played some scintillating football that sees beautiful combination play with the Dutchwoman a central part of it. But there is only one player who really captivates the minds and hearts of people with her surging runs and aggressive shots. In Pernille Harder, we've seen a birth of a hybrid number 10 who possesses the qualities of every type of role. Some would say that she is the ultimate number 10 and arguably the world's best and most consistent player in women's football, but let's allow the analysis to tell the tale.

Taking it a step back to her days at Wolfsburg, she mainly operated as a striker or second striker in a 4-4-2 and an attacking midfielder in a 4-2-3-1 formation. *Figure 29* is Harder's heat map from her final season at Wolfsburg which suggests she prefers playing right behind the striker. Her movement tendencies are very much of a player who operates in and around the box with movement in and around her.

[Figure 29]

The role of the 'raumdeuter' or 'space interpreter' is reserved for players who have an adept understanding of time and space. The role has been mostly attributed to Thomas Müller, but Harder can also be tagged as she's one of the best users of space. The Bayern Munich attacker's style of play created the role coming from his excellent understanding of space and its utilisation. While Harder doesn't fit the role exactly, many aspects of her play are reminiscent of the Bavarian striker, especially in her understanding of said space and how to use it. She is a hybrid of a number 9 and 10, which could be best described as a '9.5' who also has traits of a competent playmaker. The Dane combines her positional intelligence, space utilisation, and attacking threat to form the foundation and core component of Wolfsburg's attacking structure. This is solidified through her 1.53 goals per 90 minutes in the 2019/20 season which yielded 27 goals in 21 Frauen-Bundesliga appearances.

Out of possession, Harder played another important role in Wolfsburg's off-the-ball tactics. The strategy changed depending on the opposition in front of them. Against more possession-dominant sides, Harder found space and looked to help the midfield press to win back possession and counter-attack. When dominating possession, Wolfsburg press higher up the pitch where Harder assisted in pressuring central defenders. The Danish midfielder also fills in gaps to close easy passing lanes and press the closest player to her. However, on the ball, the other players made sure that they got the ball to Harder and there was an almost over-reliance on her. Teams would attempt to man-mark her and keep her out of the game, but because of their dominance for several years, Harder was able to put Wolfsburg through as the leading star with a superb supporting cast.

At Chelsea, the ask is slightly different. She's gone from being the main focal point to one of several. The real difference here is how much more out-of-possession work Harder needed to take on. At Wolfsburg, the team was built to maximise Harder's strengths and while she did contribute to Wolfsburg's press and overall structure, much of that work was done by the supporting cast. Lena Oberdorf and Ingrid Engen behind Harder meant she had the freedom to attack without getting too bogged down by the defensive work and much of the hard running was carried out by them.

Alexandra Popp, Ewa Pajor, and Fridolina Rolfö are all excellent players but were possibly just a shade under Harder's quality to provide the cutting edge in the bigger games. In theory, the move to Chelsea should entice more out of Harder given the onus isn't on her alone to deliver, as there are now several other high-quality players around her to step up if and when needed.

Harder's role at Chelsea sees her involved in more than just the final third both on and off the ball. Harder is deployed as number 10, centre-forward, or even a winger depending on the formation used. Inherently, the 'raumdeuter' is a free role in which the player finds space to operate, which in Harder's case remains the same. In either scenario, she is the one to drift into the central areas to influence proceedings and take control of the game. Her responsibilities include facilitating the build-up to connect the midfield and attack to create space for the forwards to operate. Harder becomes the focal point or rather reference point for the team to play through. In almost every attack, the ball goes through the Danish midfielder whether it be through a pass to feet or a string of interchangeable passes with the centre-forward. Here, her primary responsibility then becomes that of creating space through her passing and movement which derives from her exceptional tactical intelligence.

When she doesn't have possession, Harder can dictate player positions because of her movement by creating overloads and as a result, underloads on the opposite side. Wherever Harder positions herself has a by-product on the other side of the pitch in the final third because teams will often try to double up on the attacking midfielder. This all results from Harder's three innate qualities that contribute to her game – positional intelligence, smart movement and chance creation. These three attributes combined have been used differently to evoke the desired results in this system. Knowing that Chelsea want to use their number 10 in a way to facilitate and unlock the two forwards inherently means Harder may not be at the centre of it all but is still equally crucial to their success.

[Figure 30]

Figure 30 is Harder's heat map from Chelsea's 2020/21 season and it is clear to see that Harder is covering more ground than she did for Wolfsburg. The deeper areas are much more active and support a lot of what's been discussed over the last two chapters.

Though there is a higher-level activity in the middle third, she hasn't sacrificed her attacking instincts and is still moving into dangerous positions to create goalscoring actions by either scoring or creating space for others around her. Part of the reason for her deeper positioning is her need to connect the midfield and attack to continue the attacking move. As mentioned, Harder is the first point of reference when it comes to taking the ball from the central midfielders and laying it off to the other attackers.

This allows the other players to move into better positions and, depending on the formation, to be used to create an overload on the ball's side. When Harder does drop, the player tasked with marking the number 10 will follow her, meaning a pocket of space opens up in behind. This shifts the balance of the opposition defensive line which starts creating small cracks for Chelsea to profit from. An example of this is illustrated in *Figure 31* which explains the practicality of this.

This passage of play is taken from a Women's Super League game against Tottenham Hotspur which highlights Harder's link-up play. Here, she drops into a pocket of space just outside of the centre circle, being marked by two players. Millie Bright looks for a forward option and

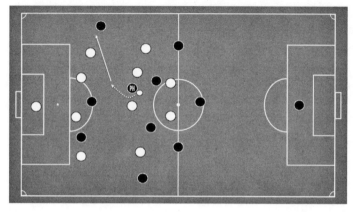

[Figure 31]

because of Spurs' 4-4-2 mid-block setup, it becomes hard to find one of the central midfielders who are pinned by markers.

Harder drops and picks up possession between the lines and evades her immediate marker, but watch how she takes the attention of four players. She immediately sends a wide pass out to Erin Cuthbert and now Chelsea have space to operate.

Compared to other wingers and attacking midfielders in the Women's Super League, Harder ranks in the 94th percentile of progressive passes received at 9.45 per 90 minutes.

Chelsea are an effective team in transition which means they're able to move the ball into the final third effectively, whether they win the ball back deeper or in the midfield. Harder's defensive contributions (which will be explained later in this chapter) aid this and when ball possession is regained, Harder is often in one of these deeper positions.

Chelsea default to a more direct style of play if they can't find a way through the thirds, so instead of a short pass into the channels, Harder will look to play a longer, more direct pass for one of the attackers to latch on to before she makes her way into an attacking position. This is an adequate method of breaking down teams that play with a high defensive line because their full-backs will naturally be placed slightly further forward than their central defenders. *Figure 32* showcases this in a game against Manchester City.

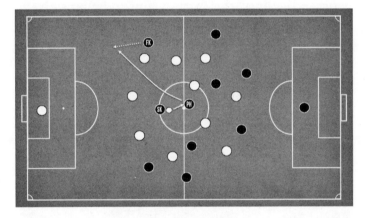

[Figure 32]

Here, a long pass reaches a slightly deep-positioned Kerr who puts it down for Harder who is in an even deeper position. Notice how high and narrow Manchester City's defensive line is, which prompts Kirby to take a position just outside of left-back Demi Stokes. From here, Harder manages to gather and release a quick, long pass down the right channel for Kirby to receive in space by using her speed to beat the City full-back. In both situations, Harder has moved into a deeper position to receive the ball, whether it be from the defenders or a second-ball win in transition.

While the first phase of Harder's involvement is in the build-up, the next phase of her contribution comes in creating space for the centre-forwards through her movement into space and where she showcases her attacking abilities. One of Harder's key strengths is her ability to identify space and combined with her movement between the lines, this forces teams to be proactive in the way they mark the midfielder. Her movement with the ball is very direct which causes multiple defenders to converge and compress the space she drives into. A lot of her movement is coming in off the half-space and moving into the central channel, however – she isn't afraid to stay wide and put in a cross or shift the point of release. The desired effect is to almost shift focus on to Harder while

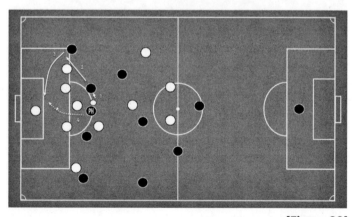

[Figure 33]

still being a relative 'ghost' by finding space. Taking a closer look at *Figure 33*, we see an example where Harder managed to do this.

This example is taken from a game against Bristol City where Chelsea play between the lines and operate at lightning speed with Kerr, Harder and Kirby interchanging positions and passes to penetrate the defensive line. Kerr's initial pass to Harder is met with an equally fast pass to Kirby. Eventually, the overload on the left side creates an underload on the right flank for Sophie Ingle to send in an unchallenged cross. Meanwhile, Harder moves across the six-yard box to find space in front of the defender. Though it didn't result in a goal, it showed intelligent movement and understanding of space to create a goalscoring opportunity.

Harder's ranked in the 94th percentile for progressive carries per 90, averaging 7.28 last season which translated into 4.34 shot-creating actions per 90 that ranked her in the 90th percentile in the WSL. The data supports the role she was asked to operate in. Hayes making her into this progressive ball-carrier and passer in a central attacking role has indeed paid dividends. She averaged an expected assists (xA) of 3.2 while delivering three assists in the league which could be attributed to her new role of being the playmaker and not the final assister.

When it comes down to it, Harder is still very much a goalscorer at heart. She contributed 16 goals across four competitions this season, which may not be at the heights of her goalscoring exploits at Wolfsburg from yesteryear, but is still a significant contribution. A critical factor in her goalscoring to her movement and positioning with and without the ball. We've already established that Harder has prime progressive numbers but it was also a method to generate shots.

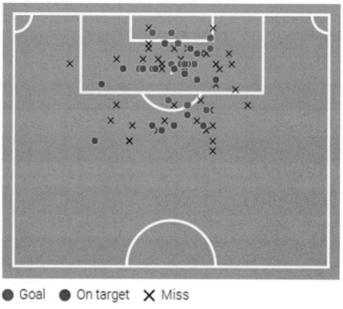

● Goal   ● On target   ✕ Miss

Showing last 75 shots, excluding penalties

[Figure 34]

Figure 34 is a view of Harder's shot map based on her last 75 shots towards the end of last season. What is significant here is the number of goals scored from inside the box which illustrates how often she makes her way into the 18-yard box. Chelsea's build-up is very direct but they do play in transition which allows Harder to make late runs into the box. Any player in a wide position could be placed to offer a cross or pull-back which Harder can meet. A prime example of this sort of movement is from a WSL game against Everton which is illustrated in *Figure 35*.

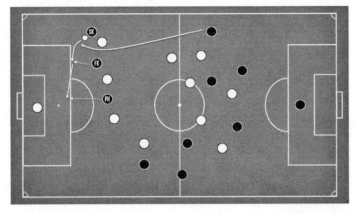

[Figure 35]

Chelsea build up through Niamh Charles at right-back who plays *that* pass down the flank for Kerr to chase which puts them swiftly on the break. A cross from Kerr to Kirby is then met with a late Harder run who receives a lay-off from Kirby and scores. This quick counter-attacking movement is something Chelsea's attacking trio were extremely adept at, given their individual qualities.

Finally, this part of Harder's game is one that has been much debated and much discussed throughout the season, one that many onlookers deem to be the part of her game that she shouldn't be doing much of. This is, of course, Harder's defensive and pressing contributions. Much has been made of how Hayes has used the number 10 position and with the increased off-the-ball contribution, there is a sense that it is limiting Harder's natural game. Surely a player who thrived under a system playing her as a deep-lying centre-forward, where everything was constructed to elicit the best out of her, would be the blueprint to follow. However, Hayes has adapted and moulded the attacking midfielder to fit into her system, which fits her purpose.

Harder's main responsibility defensively is her pressing movements. Chelsea use their forwards to create pressing traps and this becomes a key component when trying to regain possession. While we will go deeper into the team's pressing tactics later in the book, it's important to understand what they do. To summarise, Chelsea want to isolate the full-backs by making cover shadow runs and forcing the ball to be played into wide pockets which then triggers the two forwards to intensify their press. In essence, this either causes an enforced error through a stray pass or they get close enough to win back possession. Chelsea use two to three formations to press, which is dependent on the way the opposition is set up. This is based on certain triggers and within each, the number 10 will have a slightly different role.

The number 10 will look to block the passing lanes in behind so any passes that do pass the forwards become the attacking midfielder's responsibility. Additionally, the player will press any ball-carriers that enter that area or pivot on the holding number 6. The system is ever-changing as it is attributed to the opposition's formation, so for Harder, the goal is to block the passing lanes and ensure that there is no easy build-out from the back. *Figure 36* shows the positions Harder will take up while the forwards start the initial press.

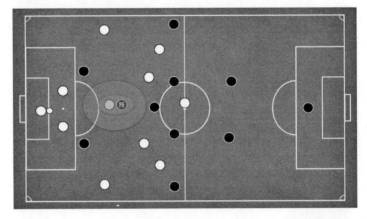

[Figure 36]

Just as has been described earlier, the attacking midfielder will patrol the highlighted area to stop the easy build-up option and press any players who enter this zone. Whether it be a central defender pushing up or a defensive midfielder placed in front of the defence, it is Harder's job to not allow them control of this region. At times, Chelsea will transform into a 4-4-2, 4-3-3 or more interestingly, a 4-4-2 diamond. In each one, Harder will perform her defensive duties more aggressively than she's ever done before.

The data is quite prevalent as seen in ***Figure 37*** and ***Figure 38***. It's clear to see that her defensive attributes have increased between her 2019/20 and 2020/21 seasons. The radars indicate her percentile ranking and if we focus on her defensive metrics, there's an obvious increase in

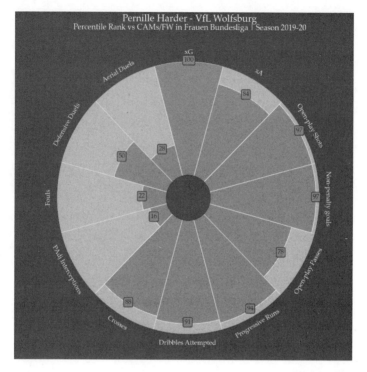

[Figure 37]

2020/21. Specifically, her interceptions have increased to 2.18 from 1.61 in her previous season which highlights her role in blocking passing lanes, but more importantly, her recoveries have also increased from 3.86 (76 per cent in the opposition half) to 3.97 (61 per cent in the opposition half). The lower ratio is down to Chelsea's press being more about interceptions than physical duels. But the overarching fact is that Harder's role has been given a bit more defensive emphasis, which is needed to make the system work. Of course, her attacking numbers suffered but she became the gateway to unlocking the Kerr–Kirby partnership that blossomed.

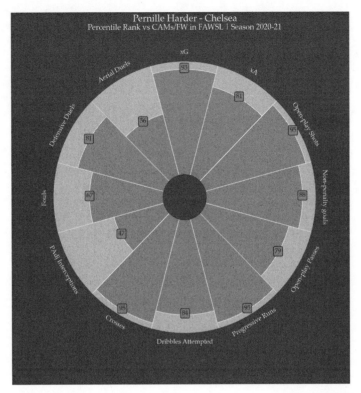

Pernille Harder - Chelsea
Percentile Rank vs CAMs/FW in FAWSL | Season 2020-21

xG
93
xA
81
56
Open-play Shots
81
95
Aerial Duels
Defensive Duels
67
88
Non-penalty goals
Fouls
47
79
PAdj Interceptions
95
84
93
Crosses
Progressive Runs
Open-play Passes
Dribbles Attempted

[Figure 38]

The story of Pernille Harder doesn't end here. How she's used in the 2020/21 season will be one of the most interesting storylines of the new season and by this point, you'll know what that is. Having reached the final of the UEFA Women's Champions League in consecutive seasons while being at the heart of two teams is no mean feat, but there is a case to be made that Harder's role could be tweaked to release more of her attacking potential. She may not be the central figurehead anymore but she still plays a big hand in their attacking patterns and movement. You could argue whether Harder was even needed at Chelsea. But it's a testament to the club for attracting the biggest talent to ply their trade in England and be part of a world-class squad. Whatever the critics and fans may say, Harder is a world-class player who has continued to show her class and elegance even in an unorthodox and foreign role.

9

Midfield Structure, Roles, and Problems

THE MIDFIELD is arguably one of the most important areas on the pitch. This is the part of the field where battles are won and lost, where many tactical plans are based. Whether it's a possession-based team or a counter-attacking one, the midfield players will control the game both on and off the ball. The evolution of this area has been obvious in the last decade where the game has moved away from specialists and purebreds to a mix of hybrids. The tactical complexity of today is such that it demands the need for a flexible midfield to the point where roles in certain midfield positions have changed drastically.

Let's take the defensive midfielder. In yesteryear, you'd think of a defensive midfielder as a hard-hitting, disciplined ball-winner who would be anchored to the base of midfield, whose sole purpose was to allow the more forward-thinking players to thrive. While this still exists, it does so in a different form. Now most managers prefer to employ a 'regista' or playmaker as the first line of defence because of the emphasis on build-up through the thirds, with the midfield becoming an integral part of this process. Having a player closer to the defensive line who is more press-resistant and excellent in distribution, especially when you lack a ball-playing central defender, means you can experiment with different build-up patterns.

Jorginho for Chelsea and Italy has become synonymous with the position and is seen as a crucial element by all his managers including Maurizio Sarri, Roberto Mancini and Thomas Tuchel. His game intelligence, passing and press-resistant nature are standout qualities that make him so desirable to lead a team's build-up, creating space and time. He also provides a passing option in any high pressing situation for defenders, so he acts as a reliever in this regard too.

The women's game has seen a similar sort of midfielder become an integral part of a midfield three and double-pivot. Barcelona have a very defined way of playing with Patricia Guijarro as the crux and fulcrum of their build-up. Her role is vital in distributing the ball to Alexia Putellas and Aitana Bonmatí who are free to push forward, given her excellent positional sense. Wolfsburg used both Lena Oberdorf and Ingrid Engen as a double-pivot and they complemented each other as a 'destroyer' and deep-lying playmaker combination. Manchester City, Arsenal, and Paris Saint-Germain are also prominent in their use of specialist central midfielders as part of their tactical plans. The importance of these players in their teams is signified by the quality of players available in this position. Every team has at least one quality midfielder who serves as an integral part of the team's spine. Guijarro, Oberdorf, Luana, Lia Wälti and Keira Walsh are all top-class players who are central to their team's style of play.

The same applies to Chelsea who have built their system to maximise the potential of their attacking players. The central duo (or trio) are facilitators to the build-up and attacking moves that enable the front three to thrive and score goals. We saw throughout the season how threatening the forward players were with the midfielders being a link between them and the defence. What we need to understand here is how the system works, the roles, and the tactical nuances that make up the system.

For Chelsea, Emma Hayes bases her midfield around progression and transition. The make-up of midfielders in her squad indicates that she wants to be possession-dominant in almost every game, which means they don't exactly require a pure holding midfielder. Each player has a specific role suited to their skillset. While there are disadvantages to not having a specialist ball-winner (this will be discussed later in the book in much more detail), the current system caters for the midfielders being a conduit for the front three.

Chelsea's basic structure is based around a double-pivot or three-player midfield. Using a 4-2-3-1, 4-4-2, or 4-1-2-1-2, they will vary their midfield setup across these systems to achieve midfield dominance, but the way they play also slightly differs based on the team they come up against. Against more dominant teams, they may opt to use three midfielders to add more pressure, but will then add a midfielder further forward when it comes to teams that will sit back. However, the midfield's main task is to facilitate and assist in build-up and support in the final third.

Chelsea have transformed from being a more counter-attacking team to a more possession-based side, but they will routinely opt for a direct route if the opportunity presents itself. The statistics back the change as we see Chelsea averaged 3.43 counter-attacks with 37.6 per cent ending in shots in 2019/20, compared to the current season numbers of 2.57 with 41.6 per cent ending in shots. So while they might be more efficient at counter-attacks, their frequency has certainly reduced drastically. The central defenders will regularly find the forward players in the channels with long passes to bypass the midfield altogether if they feel there is a better attacking opportunity. So where do the Chelsea midfielders come into play?

There is one ball progressor, one box-to-box midfielder, and if there's a third midfielder, a ball recycler who plays at the base of the diamond of a 4-3-3. The progressor is often the press-resistant one who collects the first pass and initiates the attacking move while the box-to-box midfielder provides a passing option and extra supporting body in every phase of play. Both players are simultaneously interchangeable but will more often than not stay in their own role. They usually opt for a double-pivot against most teams given their possession dominance, but against some of the more threatening teams, they'll move to a three.

This gives them an extra body in midfield to overload or to match the opposition because of the quality they likely possess. Due to the profile of players in this system, quick passing interchanges becomes a much-used option to try and play their way out of trouble but their focus is on efficiency until it gets into the final third. Let's explore their setup and movement in build-up.

Their structure is very methodical when it comes to progression through the thirds, starting with their build-up. Hayes wants her midfielders to be positionally sound, tactically intelligent, and refined in possession. On the training ground, Hayes will encourage and challenge her squad to solve tactical dilemmas to promote problem-solving on the pitch, giving them a better tactical perspective and enhanced decision-making. On the pitch, the central midfielders will position themselves in front of the back four but in a position between the full-back and centre-back. It allows the ball-playing centre-back space to step up and play a long diagonal pass (if available), and because Chelsea want to play through the half-spaces, they look to receive in those areas. From here they can push up and use overloads and multiple passing options to pass in the exterior or interior channels. We know their goal is to go out wide before coming back into the half-space in the final third which is a likely choice.

Figure 39 is a depiction of this typical Chelsea build-up where you'll see both central midfielders positioned in parallel, either side of the central defenders to receive in space. From here, the players will attempt to find a wide

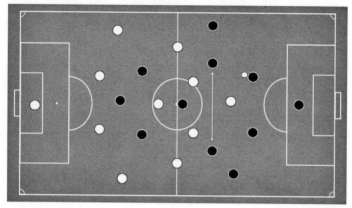

[Figure 39]

passing option into a marauding full-back to find the width and move the ball quickly into the final third. They want to progress the ball quickly so fewer passes are attempted in order to achieve this. *Figure 40* is a passing network from the 2-2 draw between Chelsea and Wolfsburg. Notice here the positioning of the central midfield duo of Melanie Leupolz (8) and Ji So-yun (10) who are both stationed slightly wider to receive the ball instead of centrally in front of the two centre-backs.

Most of Chelsea's build-up will come down the left given that Ji plays on the left of the double-pivot while Jonna Andersson is better going forward. Ji and Leupolz are both dynamic presences with excellent passing ranges, but Ji is probably one of the best passers in football so naturally, she becomes the central focus around which they build out from. Coming back to it, what's most interesting about their structure is the positioning of both players. It's very lateral, and what I mean by this is that they stay in the

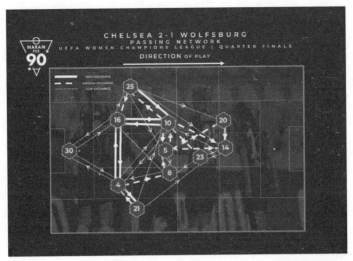

[Figure 40]

same line, maintaining a flat shape in front of the back four to ensure there is enough protection and alternate passing options similar to what we saw in *Figure 39*.

Both central midfielders have a role to play off the ball which isn't exactly pure defending but rather their role is to cover spaces vacated by the flying full-backs. Usually, Chelsea will push one full-back up to attack while the other will hold her line and provide an extra defensive presence when Chelsea attack to provide balance. In this time, the non-active midfielder will be positioned in what could be referred to as the space between the full-back and central midfielder in the defensive half-space.

As the full-back bombards forward, the midfielder needs to stay back to cover the space while the transition is happening to protect themselves from any potential counter-attacks. As *Figure 41* illustrates, the movement

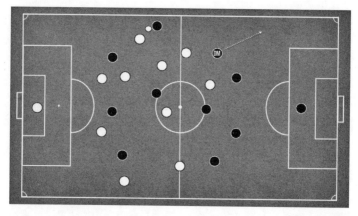

[Figure 41]

forward forces players to start making triggered movements into space to start the final third patterns, but while the ball is still in midfield, the central midfielder needs to stay slightly behind to ensure they aren't fully exposed when it comes to being counter-attacked. Chelsea don't have an active defensive tactic because their idea is that by keeping more possession, they have to do less defending off the ball. Most of the midfielders' defending comes from swarming and pressing players as they go into Chelsea's half. The box-to-box midfielder – usually Leupolz – is the player with the energy and drive to be able to be in those defensive positions and moments to try and instigate these repossessions. The problem that stems from this is that defensive gaps that should be filled in by midfielders can be left open, which allows the opposition to exploit space and beat their player in one-on-one situations.

Another added reason for their low defensive output is the way the team presses in open play. The forwards aim to isolate and pressurise the opposition defenders which forces them to go long. The resulting long ball ends up being won by the defenders and they start the attacking process again. This leaves less defensive work to be carried out by the midfielders who are much more attack-minded than defensive.

The last major role the central midfielders play is their supporting role in the final third. In general, you'll find the progressive midfielder closer to the front three to provide the pass that unlocks the move to begin the attacking move in the final third. Their main task is to unlock the overlapping full-back, which brings them into play while also maintaining their position in the half-space by forcing the opposition to protect the central areas. The progressive midfielder is intelligent enough to find pockets of space to get into a position to find the right pass. If this is executed correctly, the full-back should be released with space to gallop and find a quick cross or cut-back.

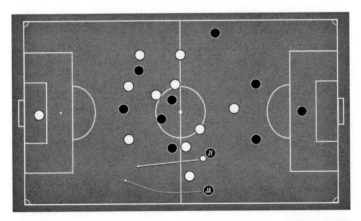

[Figure 42]

Let's take this example against Everton in the WSL shown in *Figure 42*. Here, Ji plays a quick one-two passing exchange with Andersson while Everton are pressing and trying to close the passing lanes for Chelsea in the half-space. However, Ji's quick thinking and turnover of possession from receiving the ball to releasing the pass is incredibly quick. She finds a gap between the Everton midfield line and enables the Swede to make a darting run down the flank into acres of vacant space to cross.

On the other side, the box-to-box midfielder will now make her way forward to provide support. This player will attempt to make late runs into the box to provide an extra body of support to the forward players in the box. There is a case for Chelsea wanting to overload the opposition box as it inevitably creates space for at least one striker to get on the end of a chance. With the constant movement of the front three, the box-to-box midfielder essentially becomes a ghost whose powering runs become an extra

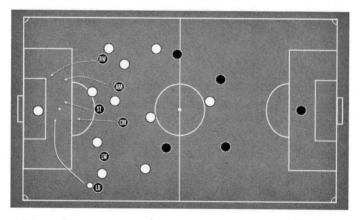

[Figure 43]

player for opposing teams to worry about. *Figure 43* is a basic graphic that depicts the sort of movement expected of the player.

Though there is a slight difference when playing in a 4-4-2, 4-3-3 and 4-4-2 diamond, when playing with a double-pivot, the two midfielders need to be more careful and wary of their movements because if they both move forward, then it exposes the space behind them. Seeing as the number 10 is tasked with more of a forward role than a deep-lying one, the onus is on the double-pivot to act as the base of the team's attacking structure. Without their work, the system fails to operate as smoothly as it does. When they do opt for a three-person midfield, it's usually Sophie Ingle who comes in as the deepest-lying midfielder, recycling possession and distributing. Her main responsibilities will include making sure Chelsea are controlling the ball when coming out of defence and linking the defenders and two forward-thinking midfielders by constantly moving the ball. However, one unorthodox tactical nuance that Hayes has used for the midfield is the positioning of the deepest-lying midfielder to be further than that of the other two midfielders.

At first, this seemed to be a random event. However, upon further investigation, this was a recurring theme in Chelsea games. One reasonable conclusion behind this could be quite an ingenious idea from Hayes. Every time the defensive midfielder would move further forward, she would act as a decoy to ensure the forward players are given a possibility of space to manoeuvre. Logically speaking, this would suggest a high probability of success because, as we've seen, the forwards thrive on space – even the smallest of spaces – so giving the opposition a distraction to carve open even more space is a no-brainer.

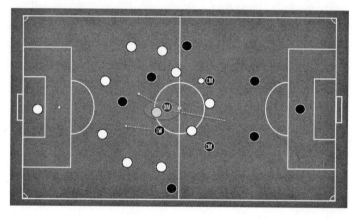

[Figure 44]

Looking at *Figure 44*; we take this example from the Women's FA Community Shield where Chelsea took on Manchester City. Ingle would make constant movements ahead of Ji and Leupolz, making decoy runs to ensure that the forwards had enough space to operate. City's defensive midfielders would have to decide whether they opt to push up to stop the potential incoming pass or hold position. Given how efficient Chelsea are in space, teams will often press them aggressively in the final third which then plays into their hands with the press-resistant nature of the midfielders.

However, Chelsea's midfield structure isn't all that it seems to be. Time and time again, weaknesses in the overall system have been prevalent throughout the season which we will explore in further detail between this chapter and the defensive one. We know that the imbalance between the midfielders has caused Chelsea's opponents to bypass them and occupy the space between the lines. Though the central defenders step up and try to bridge the gap between the midfielders and themselves, having both full-backs flying forward with no real defensive-minded midfielder has opened a lot of gaps. This has left the defence exposed to waves of attacks and against better sides, they rode their luck for most of the season but were eventually punished. Barcelona arguably exposed this perfectly through the efforts of Lieke Martens, Jennifer Hermoso and Caroline Graham Hansen, who each isolated their markers and took them on in one-on-one positions. Hermoso's false nine role was integral to pulling defenders out of position and exploiting the spaces between the midfield and defence in the UEFA Women's Champions League Final. The wingers almost toyed with their full-backs, beating them for pace with no real support from Chelsea's wingers or midfielders at the best of times. Even Wolfsburg and Bayern Munich had their moments, with Wolfsburg winger Fridolina Rolfö getting the better of Niamh Charles in the first leg of their UEFA Women's Champions League quarter-final.

Chelsea's defence relies on high ball possession and defending off the front foot. Though Millie Bright and Magdalena Eriksson are competent defenders, they aren't totally convincing in one-on-one positions, rather they thrive when cover is around to be able to step up without fear of giving up their position. And of course, we have to mention how Ann-Katrin Berger has been solid between the posts and has bailed the team out on several occasions. We'll touch more upon the defensive issues later, but the fact of the matter is that without a specialist 'destroyer', Chelsea have struggled and will continue to struggle against top-class sides.

The current midfield balance leaves Chelsea too exposed against better sides because ball possession will be even, if not in favour of the opposition. Picking Ji is probably where some of the issues lie because of the similarities in playing style and role with Pernille Harder. Both players want to attack similar areas of the pitch and carry out similar tasks which just doesn't work for the balance of the side. Ji is excellent going forward but this system only has room for one progressive playmaker, and not two. Though that isn't Harder's exact role, the emphasis on having a dynamic front three means the middle of the park needs more industry from the players there.

While the overall system and structure seem very straightforward, the levels of execution and attention to detail required are extremely high. The intelligence needed to know the roles and timing becomes critical, with even the smallest moment making a difference. Hayes has devised a scheme to ensure that the complexity behind creating goalscoring chances is supported by an equally complex, yet simple methodology run by intelligent players. Superclubs in Europe have based their success on their midfield because it provides a base from which the defence and attack can operate. When you look at Barcelona's trio of Alexia Putellas, Aitana Bonmatí and Patricia Guijarro; or alternatively Olympique Lyonnais's Saki Kumagai, Dzsenifer Marozsán and Amandine Henry; they were all crucial in their execution and they have influenced their sides' defensive and attacking tactics. Therefore, it is little wonder that Chelsea's most tactically intelligent squad members happen to be their three central midfielders. Knowing how each one of them operates is our next call of action as it'll give you, the reader, a deeper understanding of the requirements to compete in a Chelsea midfield.

10

Ji So-yun

'Ji was the focus of Chelsea's left-sided dynamics in 2020/21, and added an edge to her role as facilitator and retainer by pinging penetrative passes in perfect synchronisation with the fluid front three.' – Om Arvind

FOREIGN PLAYERS gracing English soil has been a staple and prevalent part of modern football. These players bring grace, technicality and creativity that has influenced and shaped the England national team players. There are clichés such as the Spaniards bringing vision and creativity while the Germans provide efficiency and industry. Japan has a league predicated on possession and that breeds technically proficient players.

Bringing different disciplines into the Women's Super League has influenced so many of the British contingent. You look at the way the British players have evolved over the years, and you can now see a core contingent of players who are clearly influenced by the influx of foreign players.

Sophie Ingle, Caroline Weir, Keira Walsh and Lauren Hemp have all been influenced by their foreign counterparts and team-mates. One player in particular, who has lit up the league and proven to be one of the most prominent figures in the WSL, is the diminutive and creative South Korean Ji So-yun. The Chelsea midfielder has been one of the most consistent players in the league and has been at the heart of her club's success for several years.

Ji's arrival at Chelsea came during a period of building and a trophy drought. Between 2011 and 2013, Chelsea finished seventh, sixth and seventh, which didn't reflect the levels the club had aspired to reach. The 2014 season saw a breakthrough, with the team elevating themselves to the top of the table. This coincided with the signing of Ji in January 2014 on a two-year contract from INAC Kobe Leonessa. Emma Hayes had caught a glimpse of the player a month earlier in the International Women's Club Championship Final which cemented her belief that Ji was the player she wanted.

Moving from Japan, Ji was worried about the transition to playing football in England with everything from the weather to the food being a complete change. In an interview with *The Guardian* in 2015, Ji talked about her feelings when she had moved to London for the first time.

'I was worried about the difference in culture and language,' she said. 'It was raining when I arrived and it was a new experience for me. I wasn't very good at English so I felt quite lonely. But the more I was here, the more I saw how easy-going it is and everyone helped me to settle in. I like London.'

Seven years later, Ji has settled into life in England and has become arguably one the best players to grace the WSL. Up until 2015, Chelsea's best league finish was second, but Ji's addition had not only coincided with a great upturn in form, but it turned Chelsea into serial winners by finishing as league and Women's FA Cup winners along with a quarter-final exit in the FA Women's League Cup. When they most notably ended up reaching the round of 16 in the UEFA Women's Champions League, Hayes saw she needed to build and move further in the competition. Though some of the building blocks of the team were already present in 2015 (Millie Bright, Hannah Blundell, Fran Kirby, Drew Spence and Bethany England), Ji's arrival represented one of the few foreign imports that formed the base of this team in the long run. Out of the other foreign players in the 2015/16 squad, only Ji remains, which is impressive considering the churn of players to mould the right squad into place. What we witness on the pitch now is a culmination of the hard work and influence the South Korean has had over this team and why she's considered the heartbeat of Chelsea's midfield.

Ji's Chelsea career has largely revolved around being the primary playmaker and progressor. The South Korean international has been Chelsea's midfield talisman for years, leading the club forward as their main driving force. Her playing style is akin to that of a deep-lying playmaker whose main responsibilities are to ensure Chelsea's midfield progression, whether that's through her ball-carrying or passing abilities. Across her career, Ji has played in both a central attacking midfield position and central midfield position where her style of play didn't differ too much because her movement patterns are quite similar.

Nominally, she's a left-sided central midfield player but you'll still see her pop up in pockets in the half-space, especially when Chelsea have control. Her heat map, as featured in *Figure 45,* has shown how active she is and how important she is on the ball. Being able to move across the pitch and influence play is a key component of what Hayes wants Ji to do.

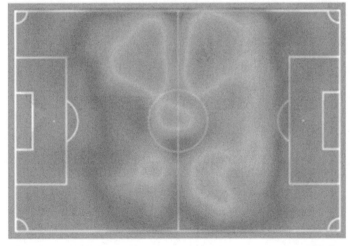

[Figure 45]

In Chelsea's various formations, Ji's position doesn't change much – rather her role will differ slightly. In a 4-4-2, she plays as part of the double-pivot and has to be much more active off the ball to cover the spaces around her, especially when the left-back will look to bomb forward. The similarities in a 4-4-2 diamond and 4-3-3 are prevalent, but overall she hovers around the same starting position. Her positional awareness is one of the world's best given her intelligence on the ball, with Ji being able to spot a pass and anticipate danger adeptly. Though she isn't so much of a defensive player, her aggressiveness helps compensate for any technical deficiencies in defensive situations.

In addition, her ability to control the tempo of the game is crucial to her role. The yellow areas that stretch out to the wide areas are where the South Korean midfielder steps forward into the half-spaces to become a conduit between the full-back and winger/striker on that side, creating overloads. Her passing range isn't limited to simple passes; rather she has a large range of creative passes as well. Ji is equally adept at using her ball-playing skill to ping long passes over defences to help break down low-block systems, allowing full-backs and wingers to penetrate in the final third.

In short, her intelligence is a core part of her skillset. This lays the foundation for every strength and attribute she possesses as it leads to positive outcomes. A major contributor to this is her decision-making, which can be classified as a subset of her intelligence. It can be argued that this is single-handedly the biggest reason for her success as a central midfielder. Players in this position have to be extremely intelligent in whichever role they opt for. Creative midfielders need to find forward solutions while defensive-minded ones need to press and tackle accordingly. Each role has its own criteria, but the ability to play it well comes from a player's decision-making and as such, their intelligence.

When Chelsea do play out from the back, Ji is the main ball receiver in the left half-space, but from here she has two options. Either she pushes forward or she finds a passing option. The option she chooses is dependent on the game situation, but it comes down to which action enables better ball progression and creates a better attacking move. Let's start with her ball-carrying abilities, as Ji has some of the best close control in the Women's Super League. Her ability to keep possession and drive forward with incredible poise and elegance is unmatched. When coming out of build-up, she's able to move into pockets of space in midfield and evade high-pressing attackers.

Ji's press-resistant nature means she can manoeuvre her way out of most high-pressing attacks. In *Figure 46*, you can clearly see how she's able to move away from her initial deeper position and get herself into a place where she can make a better decision to help ball progression. This example from Chelsea's game against Bayern Munich shows an example of Chelsea's quick and direct method of building out from the back, where Sophie Ingle and Ji combine with a series of passes before Ji is able to receive and go beyond the Bayern Munich attacker and drive forward with power, leaving a couple of players in her wake.

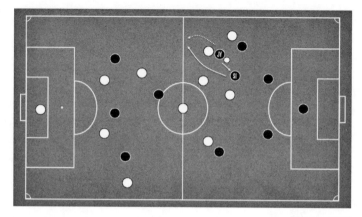

[Figure 46]

Simultaneously, it's this sort of dribbling ability that has helped her to get out of tight and high-pressure positions to then get herself into excellent goalscoring situations. Ji averaged 2.20 dribbles per 90 minutes across the 2020/21 season but most importantly, she did these with a 57.9 per cent success rate. So while her frequency isn't as high as some of the league's attackers, her efficiency and effectiveness in this regard are very high. A lot of teams will play with aggression to try and cut off Chelsea's supply, and that starts with Ji. In *Figure 47*, we can see an example of her picking up possession in zone 14, outside of Manchester United's 18-yard box where she makes a quick burst forward and drives past two players in a tight space before unleashing a shot.

In her mind, she always wants to receive the ball, her every move finding a better and more effective angle to pass or space to dribble. Though she is press-resistant, her intelligence comes from the fact that she wants to

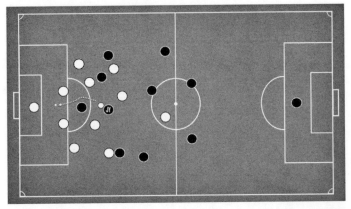

[Figure 47]

create space to dribble into, rather than having to slalom past players. However, if she doesn't have a clear ball-carrying option then her creative passing range comes into effect.

Ji's role as a playmaker also includes her diverse passing range. Traditionally, Ji has always been Chelsea's most creative player, and she still is to some extent, but the shift in focus from her being the centre of Chelsea's creativity has come with a change in system to incorporate the front three.

Now playing from the double-pivot, Ji is tasked with controlling and progressing play from deeper in midfield with Pernille Harder taking up the number 10 role. Her vision and creativity are second to none and Ji has a knack for being able to find solutions and passing options much quicker than most. Her passes can be as simple as quick, recyclable passes to long-range balls that penetrate opposition defences, and everything else in between. This range enables her to control the tempo of the game and dictate the flow. If Chelsea need urgency, she's usually the spark to provide it.

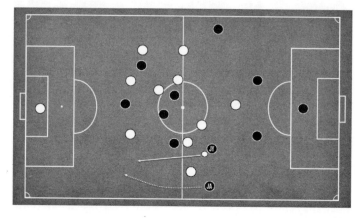

[Figure 48]

The example in *Figure 48* shows Ji's intelligent playmaking against an Everton team who tried to pressure Chelsea from build-up. Chelsea were looking to build out from the left half-space with Jonna Andersson – the left-back – looking to make an overlapping run into space around the Evertonian full-back. When Ji picks up the ball, she is then met with a marker and three players covering any obvious spaces. The South Korean manages to find a narrow path and times her pass perfectly, which carves Everton open and puts Andersson through.

The level of vision required to spot the pass is one thing, but the intelligence required to identify and make that decision quickly is extremely high. Teams from the lower end of the Women's Super League will usually deploy a low-block defensive system to ensure they don't allow opposition forwards the space to operate freely especially aerially, which is where Ji's intricate passing comes into play. In fact, teams that play with a high defensive line will be better able to cope with most ground passes because of their aggressive and pressing tactics. The quality of the player makes a difference so it requires a different type of pass. Even from long range, Ji can spot passes that few can, and even fewer still that can execute them consistently. The forwards will have to be more mobile and aware of their movements, especially when Ji can use her range of passing to send something forward in an instant. She averaged 4.20 long passes per 90 minutes (42 per cent success rate) and 9.42 passes to the final third (75.2 per cent success rate). Both metrics are extremely impressive given the quality of teams and the tactics of the teams she has to come up against. Ji's high accuracy rates are over and above what you'd expect from a player that attempts a high volume of passes.

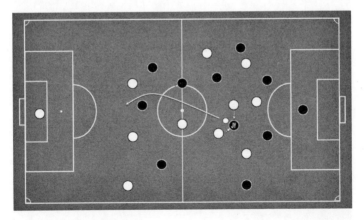

[Figure 49]

The graphic in *Figure 49* is taken from a passage of play against Barcelona in the UEFA Women's Champions League Final where Ji was under the most pressure, given the circumstances that followed in the game. Barcelona's trio of midfielders dominated but Ji and Chelsea still had their moments. This passage of play saw her pick up a pass from Magdalena Eriksson before being converged upon by two Barcelona midfielders. Within five seconds of receiving possession, she's able to release a long pass over Barcelona's defensive line and give Sam Kerr a chance to run in behind. This chance may have only yielded a 0.06 xG, but the move was created because of the quick thinking and accurate passing of the South Korean. As the game situation was dire, chances were hard to come by so the data doesn't paint a full picture, meaning that even a chance like this was a welcome sight for Hayes.

[Figure 50]

Let's bring back the heat map from the earlier chapter in **Figure 50.** The point of this is to articulate and show you how important Ji and the midfield have been over the last couple of seasons. Chelsea use those central zones near zone 14 a lot more compared to other teams. Some lighter spots in the deeper half-space areas are long balls over the top or through balls which can be attributed to what we've already discussed in this chapter.

Though for all of Ji's excellent work on the ball, there is what seems to be the eternal question of balance of Chelsea's midfield. There is a school of thought where Ji offsets the balance of the side because of her clashing style with Harder. The two players are extremely creative but are required to be proficient off the ball. Hayes demands the hard graft from her forwards and at the time of writing, Harder is the better player at carrying this out.

Ji doesn't only have an effect on the ball, but rather she has a big role off the ball too. Chelsea's off-the-ball tactics are based around creating pressure from the front while the midfield moves across the pitch to support pressing opportunities. When Chelsea go into their 4-4-2 shape out of possession, they do so to create two blocks of four where the midfielders will look to stop any passing lanes but also press the ball carriers to not give them time on the ball. Ji is deceptively mobile and has some good numbers when it comes to duels and recoveries considering her creative role. This playmaker's job is to create pressure and force teams hovering in midfield to make a decision. Given her experience, Ji is able to engage in duels and be a nuisance.

The data supports how undervalued she is as a defensive presence – having averaged 17.02 duels per 90 with a 51 per cent success rate, 4.71 interceptions per 90 and 8.41 recoveries per 90 (59 per cent opposition half). While these numbers give a good indication of how Ji has been able to contribute out of possession, her way of playing to the naked eye still shows flaws in the system for the player.

Ji wants to play in the same spaces as Harder and is more comfortable taking the ball forward as an advanced playmaker rather than a deep-lying progressor. The problem then is that the double-pivot lose some balance because neither Ingle nor Leupolz are active defenders, even though they might be positionally sound. When a system is focused on facilitating a forward line such as the one at Chelsea, the midfield has to be more industrious and solid. Having a ball progressor to link defence and attack is important, but it has to be done with a player that is more balanced in role and playing style. Ji's defensive numbers are proficient, but it's no secret that she wants to be further forward without the burden of having to carry out these defensive duties. This isn't to say Ji is a bad player, rather she just doesn't exactly fit the system in its current form. We'll look at possible solutions later in the book to discuss where and how this can be resolved.

Ji has been the bedrock and fulcrum of this Chelsea team since 2014. Racking up over 180 appearances for the club, Ji's influence is truly second to none. Hayes has changed formation over the years, but Ji's presence and role in the team have been consistent. In an article written on The Athletic, Katie Wyatt discusses how the Chelsea players were worried about the effects of Brexit, and one of the main concerns was whether Ji would be able to stay. If that's one of your team-mates' main concerns then you know how influential and beloved Ji is to the team. The South Korean may not be the modern and luxurious archetype of an attacking player that a Harder or Kerr represent – she's instead an integral cog in an otherwise well-oiled machine and the one player who brings all the qualities needed to complete a supreme European team.

11

Melanie Leupolz

*'The glory work is done from the pass later
on which is why I don't think she gets enough
credit. She's technically really good and she
does all the basics right, which is something
else that's underrated and under-appreciated
in football.'* – Alex Ibaceta

CHELSEA'S ACQUISITIONS since the 2019 summer transfer window have been shrewdly led by chief negotiator Marina Granovskaia and head coach Emma Hayes in a bid to solve the last few pieces of the jigsaw puzzle. They scouted and picked up Norwegian sensation Guro Reiten and later added Sam Kerr who brought star power and depth to an already impressive forward line. While these forward signings grabbed the headlines, Chelsea continued adding to their squad in the summer of 2020 with even more impressive signings. The quest to reach the summit was in full pursuit as we saw them add Wolfsburg,

Pernille Harder, but more importantly, they also bought Bayern Munich captain Melanie Leupolz. The German international is far from just a functional player as her skillset brings a much-needed calmness to a side that is brimming with explosive talent. So who is Leupolz?

The secret to nearly any successful athlete's career is hard work, dedication and – most importantly – enjoyment. When Leupolz was 14 years old, she played for a boys' football team and her coaches saw her potential, envisioning her to play for the women's national team someday. Her reaction was laughter. Football was always a hobby for Leupolz, with politics and film being her main interests. Her parents were her role models with football taking a back seat. Fast forward to today, and Leupolz is a serial winner having won the Frauen-Bundesliga, European Championship, Olympic gold medal, Women's Super League and the Continental Cup, after playing a pivotal role for Germany, Bayern Munich and Chelsea.

Bayern Munich were once the queens of the Frauen-Bundesliga, but even during Wolfsburg's dominant period Leupolz had been a core component, driving their rivals close year after year. She was also captain which meant that she led from the front, and it gave Chelsea yet another international captain in their ranks. The men's team throughout the years housed the captains of Ivory Coast, England, Spain, Czech Republic and Germany to name a few. When she first arrived in England, Leupolz joined some notably high-profile and influential players in the team, including Sophie Ingle, Magdalena Eriksson and Pernille Harder, who are either captains or have a big influence on their international sides. We know that Hayes is always looking for the right personality for her squad and Leupolz seems to be a perfect fit.

An ever-present member in this Chelsea team for her first season, the German largely had a good start to life in London, but she faltered at the final hurdle when she was hauled off at half-time in the UEFA Women's Champions League Final. That puts a small dent in an otherwise impressive season. Any team that wants to build a squad capable of dominating Europe akin to Olympique Lyonnais will need serious depth and balance. Leupolz is a player that adds quality, technical ability and – most importantly – simplicity. The German does the simple things so well that she almost goes unnoticed at times. This chapter will give you a better read on what qualities Leupolz possesses, and how that's contributed to the shape of the squad in their quest.

At the forefront, Leupolz doesn't seem to fit a particular role of a central midfielder. She isn't overly athletic, neither is she a destructive midfielder. Creatively she's decent at best, but when you watch her play you can see the influence she has over proceedings. The best way to describe Leupolz is that she's a supporting defensive midfielder who plays a box-to-box role, contributing to both attacking and defensive thirds without over-committing to either. Though she plays deeper, the German midfielder provides balance, energy and drive into Chelsea's central area, ensuring they aren't lacking a presence in midfield.

Partnering Ji So-yun in the double-pivot, Leupolz's main role is to ensure she provides both attacking and defensive support. She does this by filling in the spaces during build-up while being a connector in midfield (due to her comfort in possession), and by making late box runs to latch on to any crosses that may come her way. The role in itself isn't overly complex, but it's extremely important to the way Chelsea play: they predicate themselves on getting bodies into the box so the forwards have more freedom to find space. As such, she is the player who facilitates the attacking moves both on and off the ball when possession moves up from midfield into the final third. Usually, she'll receive possession from one of the defenders or midfield partners and look to create an attacking move with her team-mates around her, but her main task is to be positionally correct to keep the team's shape and balance.

Simultaneously, Leupolz is one of the alternate targets when it comes to crosses because she's a very effective aerial presence. The midfielder becomes very useful at both attacking and defending set-pieces. It's a testament when a player of this ilk is almost an afterthought because of the ghost-like effect they've had on the game and team. Leupolz's game is based on her spatial awareness and positional intelligence, which form the basis of her overall game.

There are no clear comparisons that can be made of Leupolz, but the closest ones in the men's game might just be Georginio Wijnaldum of Paris Saint-Germain and Saúl Níguez of Chelsea. Both players are box-to-box, energetic midfielders who have more of an influence off the ball than on it, yet they are proficient in their passing and dribbling abilities as well. It's very hard to pinpoint their exact contributions because the data doesn't give a true reflection, but it's the finer details you see on the pitch that make all the difference.

This role requires energy, intelligence and understanding of space which fuel her immense running, dribbling and ability to make the right decisions. Even when she's playing as part of a midfield two, she usually switches between a pure number 6 or attacking 'free 8' in Chelsea's hybrid 4-4-2 system. Her responsibilities are split into what she does on the ball and off the ball, though it is the latter where we see a bigger impact. Next, we'll explain her out-of-possession attributes followed by her in-possession ones.

While Ji is the primary outlet in build-up, we know Leupolz will be a supporting figure. Leupolz's primary role and contribution is to be a supporting player by being a passing option and a source of defensive cover. Chelsea will dominate possession in most games but are still wary of teams who will look to press or dispossess them in midfield. The full-backs in this system tend to push up higher, especially on the right especially since Niamh Charles was moved to right-back, so having Leupolz in the vicinity allows the team to move fluidly forward in the build-up with defensive cover. When the full-back pushes up, Leupolz will move into the space halfway between the full-back and defensive midfield spot to ensure there is sufficient cover in case of a counter-attack.

Here you can see Leupolz positioned in a deeper area on the right side while the full-back(s) push up. This movement combined with the positioning means the full-backs can take up higher starting positions, giving Chelsea more players in the wider areas during build-up – a key part of their process. The 'out-to-in' method of building up demonstrates how the team have to ensure they transition smoothly and quickly between the first two thirds, so having sufficient cover in defensive spaces is critical. This is similar to the example used in the midfield structure chapter.

The first ball is most often given to Ji if the centre-backs attempt to play out from the back (with the other option being a direct diagonal ball into the channels), which is dictated by the positioning of the two central midfielders. They are usually positioned in parallel to add a solid block in front of the back four. This again comes as a way to push

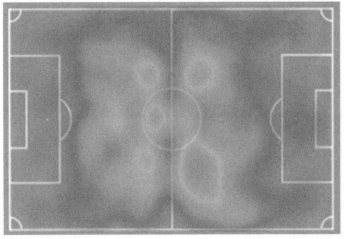

[Figure 51]

151

the full-backs into higher positions. Due to the balance in midfield, Leupolz is the primary source of defensive cover due to her relentless energy and intelligent positioning.

Her movements and overall energy are even more prevalent in the heat map which tracks her most active areas of occupation (*Figure 51*). The graphic indicates that Leupolz is extremely active in both halves, not fully committing to either box but playing a major role in between the thirds. Though this may not separate how much she was on or off the ball, it still supports the notion that her game is based on box-to-box-style movements. In midfield, Leupolz's movements and positioning are similar because it encourages space creation through intelligent runs. This is the point where Chelsea will start to face pressure from opposition midfielders through man-mark pressing strategies or solid blocks of three, four, or even five midfielders, making it very difficult to penetrate.

While Ji will be responsible for unlocking defences, it is because of Leupolz's efforts that spaces will start to open up which makes Ji's job that much easier. When you consider that Chelsea's midfield is responsible for being a conduit between defence and attack, and creating space for the forwards to operate, movement and positioning become vital aspects of their game. Leupolz has to make quick decisions and choose whether she needs to make an off-the-ball run or be available for a certain pass. There are many interactions and combination plays that happen in the half-space and while Leupolz may not be the initiator or on the receiving end, her part in linking these together through movement is just as important.

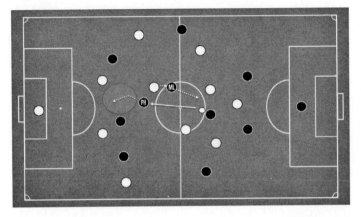

[Figure 52]

So if you look at **Figure 52**, you'll see how small movements can make a big difference on the pitch. Leupolz's move towards the right half-space means her closest marker needs to move across and follow her, but this leaves enough space for Chelsea's number 10 to drop into the space to receive a pass because of Leupolz's intelligent movement. What's made her so successful over the years is her ability to execute this role with diligent consistency. Even at Bayern Munich, she was a constant threat despite playing a very simple game.

Being the midfield counterbalance, Leupolz's defensive contributions are much more about being in the right place at the right time. A lot of Chelsea's defensive system is based on a high press by the front line which then transforms into collective movements and 'swarming' players if the ball reaches the defensive third. The first line of the press is applied by the forwards that are then supported by the midfielders to sweep up anything that comes in behind. In this case, Leupolz acts as one of the extra supporting bodies that will pressure the ball carrier and try to make an interception. This also applies to any aerial deliveries that come the way of Chelsea's box. The former Bayern Munich midfielder is a proficient force in the air, which counters a regular go-to opposition tactic.

Her defensive output reads as follows – 3.22 tackles per 90 minutes (87th percentile), 20.81 pressures per 90 (69th percentile), and 1.39 interceptions per 90 (54th percentile). Across these three defensive metrics, you can see that she's placed in the middle of the pack when compared against other midfielders in the WSL. However, if we break this down even further we can reveal a bit more information. Her tackles and pressures attempted in the middle third put her in the 95th and 94th percentile, which indicates that she is in the top five or six per cent of active presences in midfield. Her success rate in pressures is only 32 per cent (50th percentile), but her tackles won puts her in the 81st percentile. Overall, the data concludes Leupolz to be an active defensive presence with a decent return considering her role. Equally, the German is excellent in the air. At 1.73m (5gt 8in) tall, Leupolz is a very capable aerial presence, especially defensively. Though she only wins 1.26 aerial duels per 90, her percentage of aerial duels won is 66.7 per cent which ranks her in the top seven per cent of midfielders.

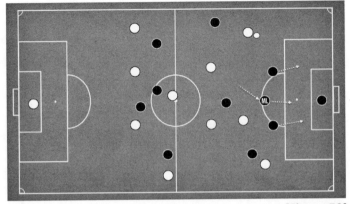

[Figure 53]

Figure 53 is just one example of Leupolz's defensive positioning and role against an opposition attack. This example comes from a WSL game against Everton where Claire Emslie launches a counter-attack against the Blues with the team scrambling to get back into position. While the defenders are making their way back, Leupolz comes up from behind while the rest delay the attacking move. Instead of following the ball that eventually goes out wide, the German midfielder instead drives into the centre of the 18-yard box and slots in between both central defenders. This gives her the best chance to defend against any crosses. Her intelligence to not run after the ball displays her intelligence in understanding the situation and being where she needs to be.

Leupolz isn't just an off-the-ball presence but a player who can keep play ticking on the ball as well. While the defensive midfielder may not be the most elegant ball carrier or passer, on the other hand, she possesses a unique ability to link play efficiently and display some neat touches in pressure situations. And even then, Leupolz is still someone who can assume the role of said ball carrier or passer, if need be. Her passing range isn't limited to simple passes – she is equally adept at using her ball-playing skill to ping long passes over defences to help break down low-block systems, allowing full-backs and wingers to penetrate in the final third. This was similar to how she was deployed at Bayern Munich. In reality, she usually plays short, simple passes to keep possession recycled but she can also play the 'quarterback' role by pinging long passes from deep if the need arises.

At Chelsea, the centre-backs Eriksson and Millie Bright will be the ones to execute that but Leupolz has this in her locker. In addition, she can make short accelerated runs through the midfield to bypass a couple of players and then release a final pass. Rather than being a specialist in one aspect, Leupolz is a jack-of-all-trades and provides across the pitch.

To help the midfield progression that involves the ball progressor and full-backs moving into the overload areas, she becomes a link player who will recycle and keep the ball moving. Chelsea can be patient in possession and try to create dominance in the central areas to allow their two full-backs space to drive forward and receive passes to create overloads. Leupolz will move between the base of midfield and the full-back's position to create a connection or pathway to ensure Chelsea are assured of possession and not liable to a counter-attack. So if possession is moved from the right side, there is another player capable of keeping it simple and progressing the ball further forward. From here, she is able to use her quick passing to keep Chelsea constantly moving and maintain their tempo.

With a player like Leupolz, putting in statistics may not be the best way to show her strengths, and data out of context is as good as not having it. She doesn't rank in the top 20 of any passing or dribbling statistics but her technique is good enough for what Chelsea need. These types of profiles aren't going to be high in the rankings but are still inherently key components of their teams.

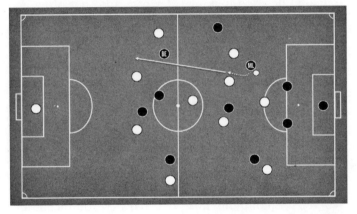

[Figure 54]

Like many deep-lying playmakers, Leupolz relies on her excellent range of passing to dictate play and affect the final third. While she is more of an off-the-ball player, she can adopt a playmaker's profile who sits at the base of midfield and plays long passes into forward areas while the attackers make runs in behind the opposition defence.

Leupolz can play a similar role if needed and when the chance does arise, she's able to execute it well. *Figure 54* is an illustration of Leupolz's passing style and intelligence in possession. This example comes from another game against Everton where Leupolz receives a pass in the defensive half-space and is quickly being closed down. She takes a neat touch to bring the ball in front of her, drives forward into space and is then faced with several players before spotting a through ball pass for Bethany England to run on to. The vision, intelligence and technical ability to make that move happen and play it quickly requires quick thinking and solid decision-making. Her passes do not often end up in assists, but rather as passes that put other players in a position to create a goalscoring chance.

Leupolz has come in and visibly improved Chelsea's midfield; given the need for quality midfielders in top European sides, the German international has definitely provided that. The former Bayern Munich midfielder has stepped up her game in what has been a bright start to her Chelsea career. Putting the UEFA Women's Champions League Final performance aside, Leupolz has largely been a staple in Chelsea's team – even displacing Sophie Ingle, who otherwise had an excellent previous season.

Chelsea's midfield problems aren't directly linked to Leupolz's inclusion, but a question of the right setup and combination comes into it. What she does bring is a wealth of experience and level-headedness that fits into the team's current atmosphere, and most importantly, she has a winning mentality having won back-to-back Bundesliga titles. After winning her first couple of pieces of silverware, Leupolz will be even more determined to be part of a team that looks to win the Holy Grail.

12

Sophie Ingle

'Ingle is a ball progression machine, capable
of taking on the complex duties of a modern
deeper-lying playmaker, whether that be
reliably starting play from the back, switching
to exploit space on the far side, or breaking
lines with judiciousness.' – Om Arvind

SOPHIE INGLE is a lady of few words, but a lot of heart. She may not be the loudest presence on the pitch, but she's one with a lot of experience and leadership. Since her move from Liverpool, the Welsh international has been a mainstay in this Chelsea side and has hardly put a foot wrong since. When we talk about Champions League-quality squads and building a team, you need look no further than Ingle. She's an exceptional talent, one who trains well and rarely complains. Emma Hayes has described her as a dream because she's exactly the type of player that doesn't need any extra motivation to train well and perform.

'But as every coach will tell you, Sophie Ingles are always players we love to work with because they do it without needing both the praise nor the kick up the backside. Perfect world scenario,' Hayes told Wales Online.

You need Ingle-type characters in your squad. It's even better when the player is an experienced professional and can come in to do a job. Her dedication to honing her craft is so high that, early in her career, Ingle would finish university lectures, train with Cardiff Met Women, and then go straight to Chelsea training. This enthusiasm and passion prompted her to be part of the Welsh setup by the age of 15.

Reading player and Wales international Natasha Harding explained to Wales Online, 'I remember when she trained with us when I was 17, first camp of the seniors, she was there as a 15-year-old girl and she was unbelievable then and has improved year after year. She's so clever in what she does. The girls respect her but she has a normal side to her, thank God – I think that's because she's Welsh!'

Her brother can take credit for introducing Ingle to football at the tender age of six. During one of his football training sessions, Ingle was seen kicking the ball around by a coach. From there, it was the start to everything we know and see. As has been the story with most women footballers, they were barred from playing with the boys in their early teenage years. This kept her out of a football club for over a year but she continued playing in the streets and at school. At the age of 15, Ingle joined Cardiff City

Ladies she would go on to stay there for five years and continue to impress. It was there that Chelsea spotted her and came calling, and the rest as they say is history.

For Ingle, it was an underwhelming season but a player of her quality will always bounce back. There is a sense that she might not be the best fit for the future of this midfield, though there is a chance of reinvention. For now, let's explore and understand what is it that makes Ingle the player that she is and the role she undertook in Hayes's system last season.

When you look at the way Ingle plays, you sense leadership, calmness and most importantly, experience. The Welsh midfielder is one of those players who play well in pretty much any position you play her in. She's reminiscent of the type of player who will give you a solid seven out of ten performance throughout a season, rarely putting a foot wrong. In past years, Ingle was one of the first names on the team sheet as a part of the double pivot alongside Ji So-yun, but after the signing of Melanie Leupolz she lost her place at the start of the season. This chapter will focus on Ingle's profile and her strengths, and on how she was used in this Chelsea side due to the changes that had occurred.

Ingle is a deep-lying defensive midfielder who is incredibly technical and versatile. Capable of also playing as a central midfielder and central defender, Ingle's profile is that of a midfield controller but she does have the skillset to play as a 'regista'. She's played as a central midfielder in a 4-4-2 and at the base of midfield in a 4-3-3 or 4-4-2 diamond. For Ingle, a place in the 4-4-2 is more similar to the way Leupolz operates where she's tasked with being the sweeper or an off-the-ball runner playing in both boxes. However, when playing as a number 6, Ingle becomes more of a defensive presence playing the half-back role, switching between defensive midfield and centre-back. By slotting in between the central defenders, Ingle then allows the centre-backs to step forward and become playmakers. This gives Chelsea a more assured way of building out when they aren't using Ji.

Playing in such a position requires an exceptional understanding of space and positioning. What she brings is a press resistance that can help to take pressure off Chelsea and combined with her passing abilities, Ingle gives Chelsea security. Her ability to attract players to her and play others in is also exceptional. She thrives in a team that plays possession-based football which allows her to control the game and is very much of the Sergio Busquets mould. Both Ingle and the Spaniard have their similarities in that their reading of the game is their main weapon with the rest of their attributes as the supporting tools. Her ability to move the ball between the thirds is great, but more importantly, Ingle is excellent in possession which means you get better control of a game. Her main responsibilities include midfield link-up through passing and creating space in possession. Her footballing intelligence enables her to make good decisions, whether it be under pressure or not.

Ingle has a good mix of attributes both on and off the ball but it's her intelligence that forms the basis of her core skillset. Receiving the ball in such a dangerous part of the pitch requires both ball skills and off-the-ball awareness. She needs to be able to understand and adjust her positioning and be aware of her surroundings in terms of player positions on both sides. As a result, this enables Ingle to either pass or drive forward and make the right decision that ultimately helps Chelsea progress the ball forward. Upon closer inspection, we see that Ingle is a very proficient passer and it's arguably her best ball-playing trait. The Welsh captain can play a range of passes depending on what the situation requires, with an ability to dictate the tempo of the game. From long-ranged passes and switches of plays to short, recyclable ones, Ingle's ability to discern when to play the right pass is unrivalled in the squad.

Her ball progression and dribbling abilities are slightly underrated given her lack of mobility, but the defensive midfielder can take the ball forward with her dribbling using subtle changes in pace and with acute movements. Though it's not a major part of her game, it is something she can do. Ingle knows her strengths and limits, and she is one of the best at utilising them to their maximum. She will not put herself in a position that will expose her weaknesses.

Figure 55 depicts Ingle's movement patterns through a heat map. This visualisation tells us a lot about what we already know about the player. Someone who patrols the central areas is mainly based in the defensive half to ensure Chelsea have cover. Ingle's activity in the attacking half can be tracked to her playing style in a three-player midfield

[Figure 55]

making off-the-ball decoy runs forward. It's important to understand her heat map in its entirety to gain a better outlview of her movement patterns.

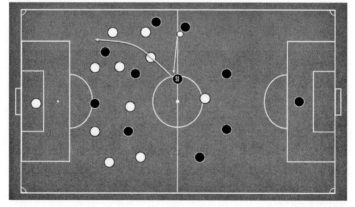

[Figure 56]

A good example of Ingle's intelligence in combination with her passing is in this passage of play against Manchester

United in the Women's Super League shown in *Figure 56*. Across many times in the 2020/21 season, Chelsea would come up against sides with a mid-to-low-block system which can be difficult to break down. In this case, Chelsea are building up through the right side duo of Maren Mjelde and Erin Cuthbert, but are met with resistance. The ball is played back and eventually makes its way towards Ingle. Now, simultaneously, the forwards are constantly moving around trying to find spaces to operate in. Ingle notices that Fran Kirby has some space at the right wing and as soon as the Welsh midfielder receives the ball, she plays a long-range pass out to Kirby, bypassing Manchester United's central structure. This suddenly puts Chelsea in a position of strength, disrupting the opposition's structure and forcing them to readjust because of one quick incisive pass from deep. Ingle's intelligence in possession shines through here because of her intelligent positioning and reading of the game.

While Ingle's 6.82 long passes per 90 minutes don't rank among the top 20 WSL players of 2020/21, it still poses a significant threat in Chelsea's way of playing. Where she does excel is in passes to the final third where she ranks fourth with 12.14 passes per 90. The only players who are better are team-mate Magdalena Eriksson, Leah Williamson of Arsenal and Alex Greenwood of Manchester City. Considering that all of them are ball-playing centre-backs who are integral to their team's build-out play and success, Ingle has registered excellent numbers showing how she's still a major influence and source for this Chelsea midfield and is the highest-ranking midfielder on the list.

Switching between the roles meant more positionally than it did to change her style of play. So when playing as a defensive midfielder, Ingle would drop back in between the defenders and allowing them to push up and ping passes. Similarly, as a central defender, Ingle would be the one to play those diagonal passes. In the absence of Millie Bright and Eriksson, Ingle was asked to play as a central defender where she used her passing range a lot more to dictate play and build-up for the team. What did change was the way she defended – using her positioning and anticipation to play a more covering role now.

Defensively is probably where Ingle struggled most in the 2020/21 season – she played nine matches across the season as a centre-back with her role more as a cover than an aggressive stopper. Being an active defender isn't really her natural game though she does provide a reliable presence in the centre of the park. In the past, Ingle's position as a central midfielder was supplemented by Chelsea's high possession stats and ball retention. The problem now is more to do with the system being slightly flawed rather than Ingle being exposed as a defender. At the risk of repeating, Ingle was almost left isolated because of having to deal with too many one-on-one battles where her mobility issues were coming into play.

If Ji and Ingle were partnered and the full-backs were pushed up, any counter-attack meant Chelsea were left with the two central defenders plus Ingle as the deepest-lying players. While Eriksson is probably the best of the lot in these solo situations, it isn't one you want your defenders to be constantly exposed to. Barcelona and Wolfsburg used the likes of Lieke Martens, Fridolina Rolfö and Svenja Huth to good effect, forcing Chelsea into these isolated scenarios.

Looking at the numbers, Ingle played 572 minutes at centre-back with numbers of 3.15 defensive duels per 90 (65 per cent success rate), 2.67 interceptions per 90, 9.28 recoveries per 90, and 1.1 clearances per 90. When you compare that with her statistics as a defensive midfielder (1,821), she had 6.18 defensive duels per 90 (62 per cent success rate), 4.5 interceptions, and 10.13 recoveries per 90. There is a clear problem in that she's having to do a lot of defending in the middle third. This has to be prefaced by saying the difference in terms of minutes between both positions is notably high, but it highlights Ingle's increased defensive contributions though it isn't an area of absolute strength.

There was a moment in a WSL game against Manchester City where this was highlighted. Chloe Kelly led City in a counter-attack and skipped past the challenge of Leupolz with the left-back higher up the pitch. Kelly was up against Ingle in a one-on-one position, putting the Welsh midfielder on the back foot as the central defender on the day. Though Ingle closed the angle for the Manchester City winger, Kelly still managed to beat her marker and get a cross away.

It's no secret that Ingle has lost her best form this season, and inconsistent starts haven't helped her cause. There's still a technically gifted player in Ingle but she isn't getting any younger – she was 30 in September 2021. Chelsea's need for a more balanced midfield can include Ingle but with this kind of player, you need to build around her rather than shoehorn her into a midfield. Ingle has been an unbelievable servant to the club since her transfer in 2018 but her future might no longer be in midfield. However, there is something to be said about playing her as a central defender in the 'libero' role.

13

Defensive Setup, Pressing and the Role of the Full-Backs

WE NOW arrive at a point in the book where we will talk about the area where Chelsea were arguably untested for the vast majority of the season, but also where there are potential upgrades that are needed to both personnel and tactics. Their defence is made up of world-class individual players, each of whom has the capability of being a world-beater on their own given day. Chelsea's back four was one of the better-looking defences in the league and Europe last season, even as a collective unit.

This chapter will dial in on the intricacies and tactical detail of Chelsea's defensive setup, system and pressing, while also depicting the role of the full-backs. This will be explained momentarily, but what's important is also understanding the potential gaps and issues that cropped up during the latter stages of the UEFA Women's Champions League, and why the unravelling against Barcelona is a cause for concern going into the 2021/22 season. Due to the nature of games they play in the WSL, Chelsea can get away with a lot without really being tested. Unless they're playing the likes of Manchester City, Arsenal or Everton, they will rarely be troubled – as seen by their solitary loss to Brighton & Hove Albion last season. Chelsea as we know are a very possession-dominant side who don't give the ball away too much. Most teams will sit back and use a low-block system which means that any time the opposition have a chance to attack, there are far too few players who can apply pressure in the right areas.

Their back four selection was relatively stable across the 2020/21 season with Ann-Katrin Berger as the clear first-choice goalkeeper while Magdalena Eriksson and Millie Bright were the first-choice central defensive pairing. Jonna Andersson and Maren Mjelde were the starting full-backs. What went from a stop-gap solution turned into a blessing as Mjelde became Chelsea's best full-back. She's nominally a defensive midfielder but her skillset is good enough to be transferred to right-back. Sadly though, the 31-year-old Norway captain was carried off on a stretcher against Bristol City in the Continental Cup Final in March 2021. That signalled the end of her season and forced Hayes into figuring out the best alternative.

Chelsea had a natural option to fill the Mjelde-sized gap in Hannah Blundell, but she wasn't afforded too many minutes upon returning from her own injury. Hayes instead opted for a couple of unorthodox options in converted winger Niamh Charles and the often-overlooked Jess Carter. The former Liverpool attacker is blessed with pace and attacking talent which Hayes wanted to capitalise on, and she did show flashes of brilliance in this role. There was rotation with Carter also coming in, but overall this changed the dynamic in how Chelsea would look to defend and attack. We'll have more on the full-backs and their roles a little later.

Defensive shape and style

On to the crux of the matter. Chelsea's defensive shapes were very situational and reactive to the opposition's initial setup. They operated with a 4-4-2 or a 4-2-3-1 defensive shape with the end result being similar, though with one fundamental difference being the way the number 10 is utilised. Chelsea's defensive output starts with an active front press. Their pressing style isn't aggressive like a 'gegenpress' (essentially a very active counter-press); rather the front line will be used to press, create pressure, and look to force the centre-backs into positions they want. The front press cannot work without the midfield operating in tandem. When the ball is forced out wide, the midfielders will step up to apply pressure along with the striker. If the ball makes its way to the winger instead, then the full-backs step forward to apply pressure there since their initial position is already high up the pitch.

When operating in a 4-4-2, the central striker and right-winger will come together to form a front two, each with a task of applying pressure to the left and right centre-backs. The idea is to stop central build-up and force the centre-backs to use their full-backs. The forwards will angle their runs to create this forced pass by covering the central space. If the opposition aren't using a specialist defensive midfielder, then the task becomes slightly easier as Chelsea's midfield will step up and act as a second line of defence in between the lines to further prevent this, as depicted in *Figure 57*.

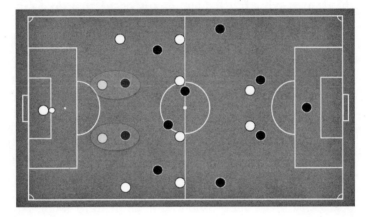

[Figure 57]

Here you can see Chelsea's basic shape up against an opponent using a 4-4-2 where the strikers – Sam Kerr and Fran Kirby – are blocking any easy passing lanes in behind while also looking to pressure the ball carrier. By moving diagonally, the central defenders have no choice but to use their wide defenders as a pressure reliever. Once a pass is made to the full-back, the near-sided player will step up to apply more pressure. The desired result is for the opposition to misplace a pass high up the pitch which Chelsea can use to counter-attack. The 4-2-3-1 is used when the opposition operates with a dedicated single-pivot or number 6. The number 10 in Chelsea's system will solely be used to man-mark the defensive midfielder and block any easy passing lanes, thus denying them an easy build-up option. Essentially, you'll see the same front press with similar ideas of forcing the centre-backs out wide but instead, there will be an extra player man-marking the deepest-lying midfielder. So any passes that do go in behind becomes the attacking midfielder's responsibility. The player will also press any ball-carriers that enter this zone, specifically ball-playing central defenders. Nowadays, teams that use a defensive midfielder do so in the form of a playmaker rather than an anchorman. Patricia Guijarro, Keira Walsh and Amandine Henry are notable examples of players who are important in the build-up for their teams, so nullifying them would create problems for the opposition and force them to adapt. As such, in either situation where a centre-back or defensive midfielder steps into the number 10's zone, it then triggers the attacking midfielder to press.

Ultimately, whether it is a 4-4-2 or 4-2-3-1, they want to form a sort of diamond formation that blocks and redirects any notion of using the central area to build up. Against teams that don't use a defensive midfielder, the central attacking midfielder will step forward and support the strikers in pressuring the defender as a cover shadow and patrol the space in front of the 18-yard box to stop any passes in behind or wandering central defenders. Another by-product of this is forcing teams to go direct. Chelsea's centre-backs – particularly Bright – are proficient in the air and can win one-on-one duels quite comfortably. Though the obvious downside is width, teams will opt to try and play these direct passes down the flanks and because the full-backs are positioned high, they're able to compete and at least distract the opposition long enough for the rest of the team to move into better positions.

Pernille Harder has predominantly been Chelsea's number 10 and has had to adapt her game to be Hayes's hard-working attacking midfielder. You would have read an extensive breakdown on her defensive responsibilities in an earlier chapter, but it's worth mentioning again that Chelsea use pressing as a means to get possession to their best ball players. Unlike some teams who utilise pressing as a source of creativity, Chelsea have their strength in attack. Ji So-yun and the front three are where Chelsea will get the most joy in attack, and having a defensive system that utilises their skillset is important, which is represented in *Figure 58*.

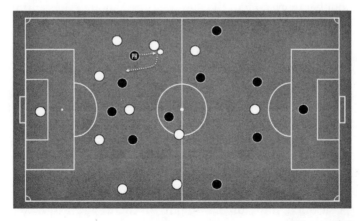

[Figure 58]

This is a reflection of how Chelsea's system looks when operating in a 4-2-3-1 system. The number 10 will ensure the opposition number 6 is not a viable passing option while the left- and right-winger will look to pressure the half-space areas along with the striker, depending on where the ball is passed to. The example featured in *Figure 58* is taken from Chelsea's quarter-final against Wolfsburg in which Harder presses Alexandra Popp once she receives a pass in the area. The Dane wins the ball back and puts Chelsea in a positive counter-attacking situation.

If the opposition manages to penetrate Chelsea's midfield and approach the back four, the team starts to engage in an 'all hands on deck' mode which means the players closest to the ball will converge on the ball carrier to try to press and dispossess. They'll look to press with two or three players trying to keep them away from the centre-backs. This works well in most games where Chelsea will have 60 to 70 per cent possession, but it becomes much tougher to execute in the bigger games. Though the central defensive pairing are competent defenders, they would much rather have cover around them and not be overly exposed to opposition defenders.

Role of the full-backs

The role of the full-backs seamlessly integrates into the overall system's tactics which are very important in the running of the system. In a nutshell, the full-backs are positioned high up the pitch to encourage a quicker transition into the middle and final thirds. If we refer back to the build-up chapter, we know that the idea is to get the full-backs into play in the middle third and see them become more of a wide crossing option and part of the overload.

Defensively, their role is to press when the ball reaches the opposition winger and to be part of a two- or three-person 'swarm' when the ball reaches the defensive third. When the ball comes directly into a full-back to engage, their aim is to pressure the winger enough to push them back towards their own goal and prevent moves in behind them. Theoretically, the more attack-minded full-back will be pushed higher up and be covered by the centre-back and central midfielder while the other full-back will stay comparatively deeper to provide defensive support. *Figure 59* shows the general areas the full-backs take up in a game situation.

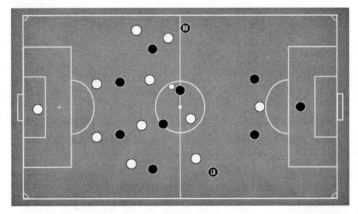

[Figure 59]

When Mjelde and Andersson were paired, it was slightly different in that Mjelde was positionally and technically proficient to get up and down the pitch, contributing at both ends while Andersson was much better going forward. A lot of Andersson's deficiencies come from her defensive positioning which is negated by having Eriksson guiding her through her defensive duties. Though Chelsea weren't as tested until Mjelde's injury, she makes a considerable difference to the team's defensive shape.

Chelsea's wide defenders have an important role both on and off the ball but they have also faced notable scrutiny from analysts and pundits alike. Ever since the Mjelde injury, Hayes tried a number of options at full-back, including Carter and Charles. The latter impressed considering she is a natural winger and certainly seems to have a future at right full-back. However, the youngster was then exposed by speedy, experienced wingers in their latter UEFA Women's Champions League matches.

On the face of it, you'd think that Chelsea's problems were majorly defensive. The team seemed to be found out in the first legs of their round of 16, quarter-final, semi-final and final matches in the Champions League, and it's undeniable that the main source of their problems came from the wide defenders. Teams were taking advantage of the space being afforded them in behind when the full-backs were higher up the pitch. Smart combination play and a lack of good positioning meant more experienced wingers were able to isolate and expose the space in behind.

This was partially down to the full-backs' high positioning, but it was also because by the end of the season

Hayes had opted to play two unorthodox full-back options after dropping Andersson. This meant neither player had the necessary experience nor positional sense to play the position as well as they needed to for the tactics employed. When going forward they can make a difference, but defensively they weren't good enough against the top sides. As has been mentioned before, against 80 per cent of the teams Chelsea face, this isn't going to be much of a problem when they hold the majority of possession. This has an adverse effect on the rest of the defence because it means the centre-back needs to come across and cover the space in behind. This has meant the central defenders are now exposed to one-on-one duels in areas they aren't comfortable dealing in.

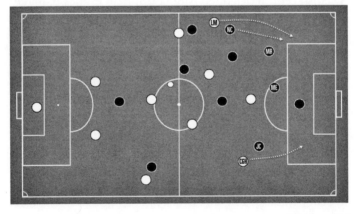

[Figure 60]

We come again to that Champions League Final against Barcelona which is probably the best depiction of a team exposing Chelsea's weaknesses. Niamh Charles was run ragged by Lieke Martens, who was able to beat her for pace and force Bright to come across.

Figure 60 is an illustration of one of the moments where Barcelona were able to use this space effectively to create a goalscoring chance. Martens comes into a one-on-one situation with Charles, beats her for pace and then gets into the space in behind. This movement forces Bright across but it opens up a huge gap between her and Eriksson. What's important here is Jennifer Hermoso's slightly deeper position, keeping Chelsea's captain at bay. On the near side, you have Caroline Graham Hansen on Carter's shoulder. Martens' pull-back into space triggers Hermoso to drop and in effect drags Eriksson and Ingle forward, but her quick pass to Alexia Putellas opens up space behind the Swedish central defender. Aitana Bonmatí evades Ji, makes a darting run into said space and scores Barcelona's third goal. The brilliant work by Martens, Hermoso, Putellas and Bonmatí created a near-perfect Barcelona goal while involving their core players.

What this tells us is that the defensive issues are not limited to the defence itself, but rather the lack of balance we talked about in midfield. Without a specialist player who can identify danger quickly and have the mobility to cover these spaces, Chelsea will continue to be exposed by teams in this regard. Teams will just try to use the wide spaces and stretch Chelsea's midfield and defence enough to utilise the space between the lines. Cohesion in this space is critical and having competent defenders in solo situations becomes even more important. Having said that, Chelsea have some of the ingredients to make up a competent defensive line, but they urgently need to do business for another full-back or two. They've already signed Aniek Nouwen from PSV Eindhoven, who will help bring depth at centre-back, but Chelsea need more. The next two chapters will look at potential solutions that could help alleviate this problem.

14

Magdalena Eriksson and Millie Bright

BALL-PLAYING CENTRAL defenders have become a norm in the footballing world. Once a rare commodity and an unthinkable role for a centre-back, they've now become integral and core parts of the team's style of play, often acting as the first creative outlet. This is common across both the men's and women's game with the likes of John Stones, Gerard Piqué, Steph Houghton and Leah Williamson all being examples of central defenders who are excellent ball players. Chelsea house two notable defenders in Magdalena Eriksson and Millie Bright, who both have their strengths and are both equally considered capable ball-playing central defenders.

The way Chelsea operate requires their centre-backs to be very good on the ball as the primary responsibility of building out from the back rests on the decisions made by both the players. Each one will assume the playmaking duties and choose whether the ball needs to be played into the defensive midfielder, or a long diagonal pass into the wide areas. The pair have played together for a couple of seasons now and have developed an almost telepathic on-pitch relationship that has made their partnership difficult to dislodge. We'll talk about both Eriksson's and Bright's skillsets and how they come together to create Chelsea's main duo while also pinpointing areas of improvement.

Magdalena Eriksson

Football, culture and politics have now become more intertwined than ever before. A decade ago, sport was a separate space that distanced itself from cultural and political issues. In contrast, sports today – namely football – have become interlinked with outside movements as a tool to help bridge the gap between societal groups and the problems they face. Footballers have become real role models, and in her own right, Eriksson has become one herself. This has come with its own share of controversy, a recent notable example being when players took the knee as a symbolic protest against racism, which led to them facing criticism all season.

We've seen excellent work ranging from Marcus Rashford forcing legislative change from the UK government to Romelu Lukaku and Raheem Sterling taking a stand against racism. In doing so, they've helped shape and change the views of the younger generation for the better. Eriksson and her partner Pernille Harder have banded together to help the LGBTQ+ youth through their chosen charity. This in itself is what makes her a role model in the women's game. Advocating for positive change and improving lives is what she sees as a result of the following and impact she has.

Sports photographer and analyst Mia Eriksson said, 'After the photo of Magda and Pernille sharing a kiss in Paris during the World Cup 2019, something "happened". For those of us who have been following both of them as individual footballers, we have always known about their open and natural mindset about their relationship. After the photo, they really added another dimension to their already strong foundation as role models and human beings. Something that Chelsea fans should be really privileged with and proud of. To have two footballers with these values that shows that it is okay to be who you are and to love whoever you want, is fantastic and something that will always be remembered.'

This exuberance – or need – to stand up for a cause has translated into her game. Eriksson has been a leader for club and country that has seen its positive effect through osmosis. Her on-pitch success and leadership effect has shone through with great poise, which only shows that she can be a success in her off-field endeavours. Eriksson has been part of Chelsea's back-to-back Women's Super League titles as well as the Swedish team that won silver in the 2020 Tokyo Olympics. Chelsea and Hayes will need the club captain to step up once again and lead this team forward if they are to become Europe's next powerhouse.

The Swede has been the heartbeat of Chelsea's central defence since her transfer from Linköping, having been identified then as a long-term centre-back for the future. Eriksson's profile is that of a left-sided, ball-playing central defender whose skillset is predicated around her immense positional awareness, ball skills and communication. These three ingredients have made her such a potent member of the squad that when Eriksson doesn't play, there's a visible void on the pitch. We saw its effect when Eriksson was missing for the first leg of the UEFA Women's Champions League semi-final against Bayern Munich where they lost 2-1. It wasn't all attributed to Eriksson's absence, though the second leg did show her significance with her making some vital interceptions. It's vital during these games that she understands and adjusts her positioning and is aware of her surroundings to ensure there is sufficient cover to not allow counter-attacks, but also to find space to pass further forward.

Eriksson's strengths revolve around progressive passing and defensive positional intelligence. Lacking pace, the Swede uses her positioning and good decision-making as a basis for her defending. Being able to judge her defensive actions early helps her to eradicate mistakes, or at the very least she's able to bail herself out of situations. She will take calculated risks but only enough to know that it's a required action.

Similar to Steph Houghton at Manchester City and Wendie Renard at Olympique Lyonnais, Eriksson's leadership qualities stand out. With several high-profile squad members in the side, the Swede sets an example for the younger players and becomes a role model for them to follow both on and off the pitch. You'll see Eriksson constantly communicating and guiding the back four and midfielders in front of her with vigorous hand gestures and movement. Her body language exudes confidence and is one of the reasons for Chelsea's stability at the back.

Eriksson is one of Chelsea's main passing outlets from the back where she's able to play both long passes and carry the ball out from defence. While traditional centre-back pairings often include a 'stopper' and 'cover', both Eriksson and Bright interchange roles with neither specifically taking up a role. The two together will rotate responsibilities with the Swede being a better progressive carrier and passer while Bright is more adept as a physical defender. Though Eriksson will step up and aggressively press players forward, the two will also take turns in doing this.

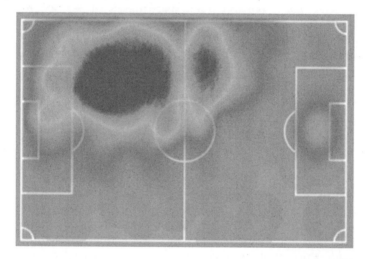

[Figure 61]

Figure 61 is a heat map of Eriksson's movement patterns in the 2020/21 season. What is most prevalent is how high up the pitch she gets. Given Chelsea's use of a high defensive line, this is how Eriksson can step forward and play those passes or carry the ball forward. Given that most of the teams they come up against will set up with a low block, this affords her the space to carry this out. She's very comfortable moving forwards and controlling the ball well with her feet. Her awareness in possession is excellent, which extends to her ability to find good passing options going forward.

Against teams that will sit back and soak up pressure in a low block, Eriksson doesn't need to find one of the defensive midfielders, rather she can go more direct and try to force the opposition out of shape and position. These quick passes can be a good way to find space in behind if the ball receiver can win the ball high and engage in quick combination play in and around. Looking at *Figure 62*, we take an example from a WSL game against Reading where the away side have taken up positions in their own half which gives Chelsea's defence enough space to step up.

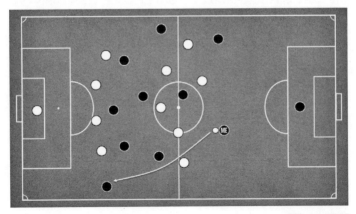

[Figure 62]

Eriksson steps up with Sophie Ingle and Ji So-yun in the vicinity but instead of going short, she sees an opportunity to play left-back Jess Carter into the vacant space ahead. With Reading's defensive line narrow, Carter can start a quick passing exchange with the interior midfielder (Fran Kirby) to try and create a goalscoring action.

Chelsea have players who all have the capabilities to play a high volume of progressive passes but it's a testament to the Swede's ability that she ranks fifth in the WSL for progressive passes per 90 minutes with 13.96. Surprisingly (or rather unsurprisingly), the four players ahead of her are all defenders, which emphasise, the importance of defenders in a team's build-up tactic. Even under ball-progression-by-minute/runs metrics, Eriksson ranks in the top five of WSL players. The strength of Eriksson's passing is only supplemented by the heavy possession-based tactics employed by Hayes given the amount of space she's allowed to use to progress forward. Teams that don't afford Chelsea the space do cause problems, but Eriksson is probably one of the better defenders that can more often than not bypass a high press.

Defensively, Eriksson is aggressive in her style of play, coupled with good decision-making to choose her moments. She's defined by her capabilities out of possession and her ability to read the game with power and intelligence. Chelsea defend on the front foot, which means she needs to be actively finding the right moment to step up and stop the striker from having time to turn and make their next move. Though Bright is also very aggressive, the two have to be wary of their positions because of how high they are positioned. Even if she does step up to make tackles and pressure ball receivers, Eriksson will not make rash decisions by flying in without making a good judgement call.

Now you have to keep in mind that Chelsea's centre-backs are not exposed to a high frequency of defensive duels so the overall volume is low. The fact that Eriksson does not feature in the top 30 for defensive duels supports this notion. Let's take the following example. *Figure 63* is an illustration of how Eriksson's able to adapt and recognise the danger to stop a threatening attack from West Ham.

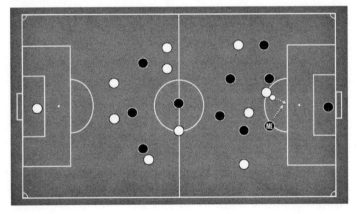

[Figure 63]

West Ham have mounted an attack through the middle with both Chelsea centre-backs marking their strikers. The West Ham ball carrier plays a defence-splitting pass for Bright's marker and when it becomes obvious that she can't catch up and engage, Eriksson moves across and goes to intercept the incoming pass. She had to make the move early otherwise she wouldn't have made it in time.

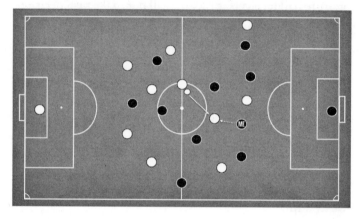

[Figure 64]

Alternatively, if we look at another passage of play in *Figure 64*, this time coming against Manchester City in the WSL, Eriksson sees City build a central attack through Caroline Weir, who evades the advances of Kirby and Melanie Leupolz to find Sam Mewis in space. Mewis's body is facing her own goal, which almost acted as a trigger for Eriksson to push up quickly and not allow the American to turn and have space to find a City attacker. The Swede manages to get an inch-perfect tackle in and ultimately wins possession back for Chelsea.

The only concern around Eriksson is similar to the one around the rest of the defence – their ability under pressure when the opposition is running at them. The team tends to move back and react deeper in the box. She isn't the quickest from a static position so more mobile players are able to get past or around her, but she's intelligent enough to work around this. There were games against Barcelona and Reading where she was ousted by their wingers and strikers in one-on-one situations, whether it be covering the space behind the full-back or centrally – as exemplified in *Figure 65*. Considering that the 30th ranked player for defensive duels in the WSL averages 8.54 per 90 minutes, Eriksson's output is just 3.51 in comparison. So you can see how seldom she has to face these moments, but concentration and protection still come into it.

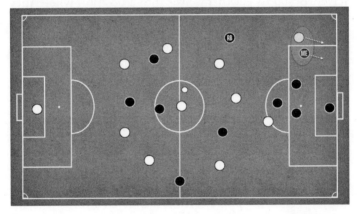

[Figure 65]

Here in *Figure 65*, you have Eriksson coming up against Caroline Graham Hansen out wide in a one-on-one situation. The Norwegian winger is an excellent player in one -on-one scenarios and uses this to her advantage. Though Eriksson starts in a good position and shepherds the winger down the line, Hansen manages to extract enough space to get parallel to the Swede and get a cross away.

Ideally, Eriksson should have stopped the cross or conceded a corner given the advantageous position she's in, with the touchline acting as a second supporting player. However, she used her experience and footballing IQ to nullify the cross as best as possible. This is where Chelsea and Eriksson have admittedly suffered throughout the season.

'[For] Chelsea to have two football players [Pernille Harder and Magdalena Eriksson] that with no doubt are among the world's best in their respective positions and roles they play on the pitch is quite telling for how Chelsea have worked to get themselves into a position where they can attract players at this level,' said Mia Eriksson.

Both central defenders are complementary to each other but what is it that Bright brings to this partnership that Eriksson doesn't? Let's take a closer look at Bright and see how she complements and stands out in this pairing.

Millie Bright

'Over the past six years, Millie Bright has become one of the best centre-backs in Europe under Emma Hayes at Chelsea. Never afraid to participate in some no-nonsense defending, the equilibrium she finds with Magda Eriksson has allowed this Chelsea team to shine.' – Jessy Parker-Humphreys

Like her central defensive partner, Millie Bright has a winner's mentality having won nine trophies since 2015.

Being at the top of her game is a culmination of the hard work and graft from her early years to reach the pinnacle of her career. It wasn't an easy journey into football. Bright had numerous health problems starting all the way back at eight days old when she was diagnosed with pneumonia, and what followed in the next decade would have floored most people, let alone a girl with aspirations to become an elite athlete. Bright was making regular hospital trips every other day as a result of asthma attacks and whooping cough which did not stop until after her 14th birthday. Once she had her health problems under control, Bright was determined to not let her breathing issues control her nor her career. She wanted to take matters into her own hands and shape her own destiny.

It could have all been very different for the English centre-half, who might instead have gone into the world of equestrianism. Her first love has been horses since the age of three, and she only stumbled upon football at the age of nine by watching a friend on the sidelines.

She realised early on that she wasn't a very good footballer but her personality is such that she took it as a challenge to still make it in the game. When football became serious at the age of 12 in Sheffield United's academy, she wasn't sure where it would lead. At that time, women's football was in its infancy and not a reliable career option because it wasn't professional. Once again, she took a risk and continued to persevere and at the age of 16 she signed for Doncaster Belles, going straight into the first team. She was also holding down two part-time jobs to make ends meet while being a semi-pro. The level of sacrifice and hard work needed to make it is phenomenal but her self-belief is probably her biggest asset. Several years later, in 2015, Bright was spotted by Chelsea and signed for them. The rest is history; we know how her career has panned out so far and if there's anyone who understands the need to stay on top of her game, it's Bright.

Despite a multitude of trophies and medals, Bright has also been recognised on the world stage by being named in the FIFPro Women's World 11 alongside Wendie Renard who, besides Lucy Bronze, has been an inspiration for her. She models herself after Lyon's captain in the way she drives her team and looks to be the difference in big games. Bright may have suffered defeat in Chelsea's biggest match, but she has shown a propensity to come back from adversity and this setback will only make her more determined to step up and push the team forward to create a legacy.

Bright's profile can be summed up in a few words – a physical and aggressive ball-playing centre-back. She's been a consistent presence at the back for Chelsea with her ability to play out from the back and defend aggressively. This type of centre-back is often used in a creative way to create goalscoring opportunities, offer a deeper passing option, and stop attackers from having time to react. Bright's main attributes are her ability to break opposition lines and relieve pressure through her passing and forward drive. She can and will step forward and drive with the ball if the opportunity presents itself. There are times we'll see her in the final third making a marauding run forward. Another added capability is her physical power and strength, making her a valuable asset in attacking and defending set pieces.

Bright as well as Eriksson will be seen pushing up to stop players coming forward, though Eriksson is slightly better at this. When Bright steps forward to stop players higher up the pitch, there is a tendency to leave space in behind that can be exploited. This is one of the reasons for Chelsea trying to block any form of central build-up from the opposition. This requires the other centre-back to be tactically switched on to provide cover – especially with the full-backs pushed up. When one pushes up the other will tend to stay behind and ensure there is sufficient cover. Upon closer inspection of her heat map in *Figure 66*, Bright's movement patterns are similar to Eriksson's with both maps a mirror image of the another.

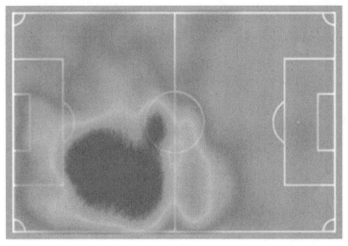

[Figure 66]

This supports the notion that both players like to push up when the opportunity presents itself, being much more comfortable in these positions which reflects the team's overall dominance in games.

So what can she do with the ball at her feet? Arguably Bright's biggest strength is her ability to progress play and create space with her passing. She is often used as a passing outlet to try and break lines of pressure and break down teams who use a low block. While she can be vulnerable to aggressive high-pressing systems, she is more often than not able to provide her team with an option to move possession forward. Ball-playing defenders allow teams to play their midfielders slightly higher and given how Chelsea's double-pivot prefer to be higher, it gives them much more room to dictate play and find team-mates in more advanced positions. The higher defensive line means the whole team pushes forward, forcing opposing teams to hold slightly deeper positions.

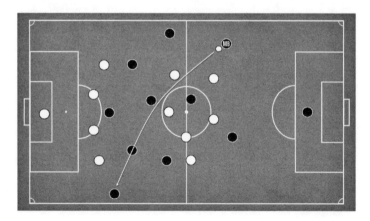

[Figure 67]

Figure 67 illustrates an example of this effect in a game against Aston Villa last season. Villa turn over possession with Chelsea looking to reset and build out from the back again. Notice how Villa's first action is to fall back into a deep 5-4-1 system off the ball, with both Chelsea full-backs pushed up and only Drew Spence dropping back to offer a passing option. The other player is Harder, who had won the original duel, making her way back up the pitch. Bright, in possession, pushes up but spots left-back Hannah Blundell in space and a chance to break Villa's compact back line. The quick diagonal pass into Blundell now gives Chelsea an opening.

Bright has also shown proficiency for progressive carries from defence. If there is an opportunity that presents itself, then Bright will push forward with the ball at her feet and alter Chelsea's build-up which forces opposing teams to adapt. When teams adopt a high or even a more aggressive man-marking press, the ability to break through these lines of pressure becomes very important as an alternative to the direct route. Every time the centre-back moves forward, the defending team needs to react to the unanticipated situation and this allows the team in possession an opportunity to capitalise. Bright can carry this out but, as mentioned, is susceptible to leaving unwanted space in behind.

Bright ranks 21st for ball progression by runs (with Eriksson ranked third) in the WSL in the 2020/21 season which, when you look at the other players on the list, is impressive. Players like Lucy Bronze, Harder,

Leah Williamson, Ona Batlle, and Abby Dahlkemper are all exceptional players with the ball at their feet and progression.

That moment can be described with both of Chelsea's defensive midfielders closely marked by Wolfsburg's forwards, and with the centre-forward Ewa Pajor closing in on Bright, she makes the decision to step forward and bypass both Pajor and Fridolina Rolfö. In doing so, she powers through midfield and forces up to three Wolfsburg players to converge on her position, which opens up some space for her team's forwards to move around and into. She releases the ball to Sam Kerr and starts a quick series of passes that creates an opportunity for Chelsea.

When it comes to her defensive duties, Bright holds a physical advantage over most of her competitors. She's a big presence who can bully most attackers and in most situations, she wins her aerial battles. She can handle ground duels but that's not where her strengths lie. Bright can read a game well, which is seen in her ability to push out and make tackles early. Bright has struggled because of some positional issues though it's mainly her lack of pace that means making a recovery becomes difficult, so that's where Eriksson comes in.

On the other hand, any crosses or direct 'route one' balls that come into Chelsea's area are dealt with quite easily. This also applies to set pieces, where she's comfortably able to deal with corners and free kicks. On average, Bright registered 3.13 aerial duels per 90 minutes with an 83.58 per cent success rate in the WSL last season. While it is a low frequency that doesn't rank her in the top 30, the success rate in contrast ranks her first in the league.

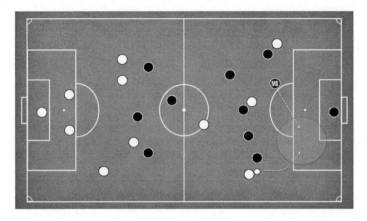

[Figure 68]

In *Figure 68*, we have an example of her brute strength where she goes in to cover the space left by Eriksson in the final against Barcelona and manages to reach the ball just as Alexia Putellas does, and shoves her off with ease. In moments where she's able to reach an attacker and get side-on, there is a good chance Bright can win the duel because of her physicality. However, in certain situations where she's pushed up to defend high, the quick-thinking, intellectual forwards can give her the slip similar to the way they get away from Eriksson.

In *Figure 69*, we have a passage of play from the same match where Barcelona launch a quick counter-attack and play the ball into Lieke Martens's feet with her back to goal. Bright spots the pass early and presses the Dutch winger. However, a quick turn upon receiving the ball sees Martens

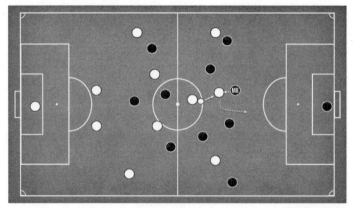

[Figure 69]

get away from the English central defender and now goes into space to face Eriksson.

These are two instances where Bright has displayed her spectrum of qualities where she's shown a proficiency to spot danger and show her strength yet has also left space in behind, leaving her defence exposed in a counter-attacking situation. Bright is clearly a good defender given that she's been the other stable presence in this partnership, but teams have started to find small nuances in their game to get through the Chelsea midfield and into the duo. There is a section of people who do not give Bright her fair due. But there aren't too many central defenders under the age of 30 that you'd bring in to replace Bright.

Chelsea's centre-back partnership is one of the better ones in Europe and *Figure 70* is a testament to that. The graphic highlights the different areas both players excel at and how it's very complementary to their playing styles. One might be a better passer while the other is a better

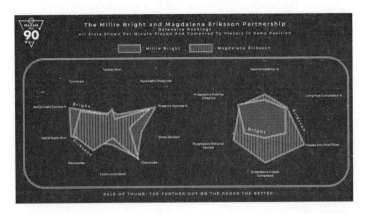

[Figure 70]

tackler, which makes defending easier and better for the back four as a whole. There aren't too many current line-ups that boast better partnerships than Eriksson and Bright. The problems are partially defensive, but the fundamental problem lies in midfield where the balance doesn't offer adequate protection to the two centre-backs. Though there are improvements the centre-backs can make, their personal stories and roles both on and off the pitch will only propel this team to reach the status of Europe's elite.

15

Maren Mjelde

'One of the most experienced heads in this
Chelsea side, Mjelde brings remarkable
consistency to the right-back position, perfectly
balancing attack and defence. Her penalty
taking ability shows just how incredibly calm
she manages to be.' – Jessy Parker-Humphreys

VERSATILITY IS a key component of any playing squad. Whether it be in a defender, midfielder, or attacker, being able to play in a variety of roles and positions becomes important over the course of a season. Though we've seen several high-profile examples such as Saki Kumagai (defensive midfield and centre-back) and Magdalena Eriksson (centre-back and left-back), there aren't many who can play three roles at an extremely high level. Maren Mjelde is Chelsea's and Emma Hayes's jack-of-all-trades star, capable of playing as a defensive midfielder, centre-back and right-back. Rather than being average in all three positions, Mjelde has instead been able to carry out her roles at a very high level. This has been a common theme throughout her storied career, dating back to the start of her footballing days.

Mjelde joined Arna-Bjørnar in Norway at the age of 15 when she started her career before moving to Turbine Potsdam of the Frauen-Bundesliga. From there, she played for Göteborg FC of the Swedish Damallsvenskan before a move back to Norway, playing for Avaldsnes IL in 2015. This would be her last move prior to making it to Chelsea in 2016, where she cemented herself as one of the most reliable players in the squad. She's very reminiscent of current Chelsea men's captain César Azpilicueta – not only in position but also in attitude. Mjelde's performances can go unnoticed and she gives her team a seven out of ten performance every single week, yet she is also one of the key leaders of the squad. Similar to Sophie Ingle, Mjelde is one of those players who just performs regardless of opposition.

Mjelde's season may not have been long but it was enough to prove how important a role she played for the first half of that season. The Norwegian midfielder was coerced into playing at right-back after a long-term injury to Hannah Blundell a season earlier. Having played at centre-back as well as her natural defensive midfield role, this move represented another shift in role and position, but one that Mjelde accommodated with precision. Mjelde's profile can be described as a supporting full-back, focusing on defending first and attacking second. Her biggest asset is her positional awareness, which enables her to take up good positions to stop attacks down the right flank and move into favourable attacking positions. This translates well when playing as a centre-back because the role demands excellent awareness and defensive intellect.

Chelsea's full-backs are not fundamental to the system but they nonetheless play an important role in facilitating the rest of the team. Though Mjelde didn't play much of the second half of the season, this chapter will highlight her attributes to this team and why she'll be critical to the team going forward. At 31 years of age, Mjelde isn't young; however, she is still Chelsea's best full-back among the current crop. As a natural defensive midfielder, her greatest asset is her combined positioning and defensive ability, and that comes from playing in midfield.

These skills have set a solid foundation and allowed Mjelde to assert herself against some of the most dangerous wingers in the league. Chloe Kelly, Bethany Mead and Lauren Hemp have terrorised defences and Mjelde performed excellently to prevent them from dominating her team's flank. The full-back position has changed in the modern game and there is a real sense that the quality of attacking players is higher than defensive ones in the women's game. However, that gap is slowly closing with the tactical and coaching improvements that have taken place in recent years. Lucy Bronze, Hanna Glas, Katie McCabe and Ashley Lawrence have all displayed high levels of creativity, defensive awareness and tactical acumen. Even the younger generation of Maya Le Tissier, Esme Morgan and Jorja Fox have started to play at a very high level at such a young age.

Take Bronze as an example – at Olympique Lyonnais Féminin, she was played as a progressive full-back who also coupled into a defensive midfielder out of possession. This is reminiscent of João Cancelo or David Alaba under Pep Guardiola at Manchester City and Bayern Munich respectively. Lawrence at Paris Saint-Germain was one of the standout players in their title-winning season, being the most progressive full-back and a source of their attacking forays. Similarly, Mjelde's role was more withdrawn which meant Jonna Andersson was allowed to play a more attacking game. The Norwegian is a defensive tactical option given her strengths there, with the added bonus that she's comfortable in possession.

Chelsea's 4-4-2 and 4-4-2 diamond is heavily predicated on the full-backs but is also a source for opposition wingers

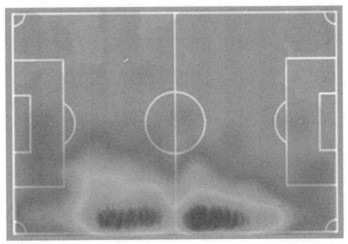

[Figure 71]

to target, so having a positionally sound full-back becomes vital. Mjelde's strengths are mainly built on her defensive positional intelligence. The Norwegian full-back's positioning is really what makes her a good full-back. Coupled with a high footballing IQ, Mjelde's decision-making ensures she keeps wingers occupied. In *Figure 71*, we have her heat map that depicts her common movement patterns.

The nature of Chelsea's defensive line means they are positioned high, so naturally, Mjelde will be spending some time in the attacking third. Though what's interesting is the slight activity in the inner channels, showing that she does come inside to defend if required. This becomes more prevalent the deeper she goes. The lack of an active defensive midfielder means Mjelde would look to cover the spaces next to her centre-half – Millie Bright – in case of overloads.

The right-back has averaged 6.64 defensive duels, winning 66 per cent of them, and made 8.78 recoveries per 90, with close to 34 per cent coming in the opposition half. While standalone statistics don't paint a full picture, the figures do indicate that Mjelde is a proficient defender in isolation. She isn't afraid to take on her winger and wants to play aggressively to ensure she has the upper hand in the duel. This has given her and the team defensive solidarity and it has forced teams to attack down the opposite flank.

Figure 72 is an example of Mjelde's excellent positioning and how it gives Chelsea defensive assuredness on her side. Here, Chelsea's back four hold an excellent line and Mjelde

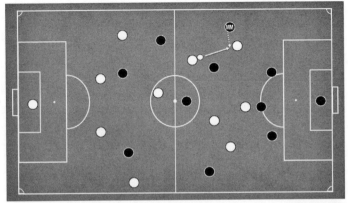

[Figure 72]

doesn't stray too far from the ball receiver. In fact, she stays close enough to apply immediate pressure once the pass is received. Mjelde steps into the space in front of her to intercept the pass before the winger has a chance to react. This not only stops the opposition from getting a chance to regroup and build an attack, but it ensures that Chelsea win it back away from their 18-yard box.

Chelsea's strategy going into games revolves around their swarming press. This is an important aspect and one that has been vital to their victories against other top-quality sides. Mjelde has been a major part of it playing as the full-back as she pushes up to press certain opposition teams from higher up the pitch. While Andersson will do similar on her side out of possession, it is Mjelde who provides the defensive balance. But what's important is that alongside her intelligent positioning, Mjelde is excellent at one-on-ones. Most defenders can cope in multi-player pressing situations, but for a full-back, solo duels are vital. Her approach has seen Chelsea able to win back possession from advantageous positions or even positions of compromise. This has enabled Chelsea to have a reliable figure in defence keeping players occupied, which can be seen in *Figure 73*.

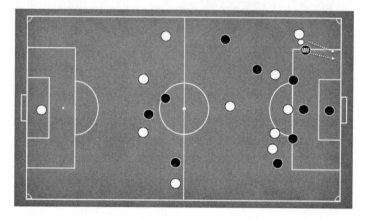

[Figure 73]

Mjelde is tracking back after her winger, who catches Chelsea on the counter-attack. There are no players in close proximity, with the closest players in the centre of the box. Maria Thorisdóttir is the nearest player to help Mjelde in case the West Ham winger tries to play her way out or cross, but the onus is on Mjelde to stop the supply. The Norwegian manages to stay upright and maintain good body positioning, which narrows down the options for the winger. She stops the cross and only concedes a corner.

This skillset ultimately transfers to any position she's asked to play in. Mjelde knows how to defend and be confident in possession. With such an impressive pass accuracy rate (88 per cent) last season, you can rest assured that Mjelde can play in any sort of system. She's a player who has such a positive impact on the squad and given Chelsea's woes in the position, Hayes will be happy to see her full-back return next season. Would she have solved Chelsea's problems completely last season? Probably not. However, Mjelde would have brought balance and experience when it most mattered. At 31, you would think that Mjelde's coming to the end of her prime as an athletic player, though with some changes in the system, there is a position Mjelde could take up to prolong her career and until Chelsea can find or promote someone capable of owning the full-back role in the long term, we may well see Mjelde keep the mantle for at least another season or two.

16

Is the 3-4-2-1 Formation the Solution?

COMPLEX TACTICAL plans in women's football have come to the fore in recent times. Managers such as Lluis Cortes, Emma Hayes, Olivier Echouafni, Jonas Eidevall and Jens Scheuer have all created in-depth schemes to outwit the opposition, which makes for an entertaining watch for fans. Last season's UEFA Women's Champions League was a showcase of these teams coming up against each other and exposing flaws that many wouldn't have been able to see in their domestic competitions. The European competition is the only place to test their abilities and truly find out who is the best.

Chelsea were second-best to a rampant Barcelona side but that is no knock on the Blues given their extraordinary performances throughout a season that still ended with them as WSL champions for a second time running. We've read about their impressive performances but also highlighted the problems. Hayes has devised a truly

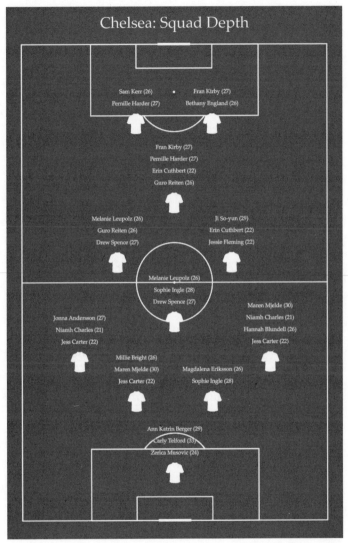

Chelsea: Squad Depth

Sam Kerr (26)
Pernille Harder (27)
Fran Kirby (27)
Bethany England (26)

Fran Kirby (27)
Pernille Harder (27)
Erin Cuthbert (22)
Guro Reiten (26)

Melanie Leupolz (26)
Guro Reiten (26)
Drew Spence (27)

Ji So-yun (29)
Erin Cuthbert (22)
Jessie Fleming (22)

Melanie Leupolz (26)
Sophie Ingle (28)
Drew Spence (27)

Maren Mjelde (30)
Niamh Charles (21)
Hannah Blundell (26)
Jess Carter (22)

Jonna Andersson (27)
Niamh Charles (21)
Jess Carter (22)

Millie Bright (26)
Maren Mjelde (30)
Jess Carter (22)

Magdalena Eriksson (26)
Sophie Ingle (28)

Ann Katrin Berger (29)
Carly Telford (33)
Zecira Musovic (24)

[Figure 74]

nuanced and thorough plan with technical complexities, but a few tweaks can truly change this team. She can be considered one of the best tacticians in women's football today. Any side chasing a European conquest will need to be a chameleon and adapt to their surroundings when the need arises. Any championship squad will need to show tactical flexibility and trying something uncommon might be key to their quest towards European domination.

If we look at *Figure 74*, which shows Chelsea's starting line-up from last season, we can see their strength – not only in the starting 11 but in their depth as well. There are several players who barely got any game time but could potentially be used in an alternative system.

Now, assuming Chelsea continue to use a combination of their 4-4-2, 4-4-2 diamond and 4-2-3-1 with a similar squad without adding in the required personnel, then I believe they will encounter similar issues to the ones we've already explained. The squad is undeniably excellent, littered with world-class players, but I think Chelsea's insistence to almost shoehorn the rest of the players into a team will be detrimental to the team's balance in the long and short term. In the next two chapters, I want to propose a tactical solution and build a starting 11 that suits the current squad. At the time of writing (mid-September), we haven't seen these propositions enacted yet, but this may change by the time you read this.

At the moment, one of the most popular tactical systems revolves around three at the back. Formations such as 3-4-3, 3-4-2-1 and 3-5-2 have become profoundly popular among coaches, and more and more teams are adopting this strategy. The women's game has seen it being used sparingly or only in the event of a tactical surprise;

there seems to be no particular team that specialises in this system. I think the 2021/22 season will see it being used more commonly, and I see it as an effective tactical option. Hayes and Chelsea would be well suited to resume using such a system because of the profiles of players they already have at the club. If the insistence – and rightly so – to continue to pursue having a front three of Fran Kirby, Sam Kerr and Pernille Harder carries on to the future, then leveraging the strengths of the other players will be important. It's not as though Hayes is new to this sort of system having played it regularly in 2017/18, but it's about identifying and recognising the strengths and weaknesses of the squad and adapting to them.

The subsequent game after the UEFA Women's Champions League Final was an FA Cup tie against Everton that saw Hayes name an experimental side playing a 3-4-3. In their pre-season friendly against Rangers, Hayes also used a 3-4-2-1 system so the thought is clearly there but let's go deeper and really understand why this is a suited system.

Part of the reason behind its low usage comes down to the lack of player profiles who can fulfil the tactical roles required. However, we have to consider the quality of managers in the past who maybe weren't as diverse in their selection. These days, with the list of aforementioned coaches and a more intelligent pool of players to choose from, there is an argument to introduce a back three regularly.

I firmly believe Chelsea can use a 3-4-2-1 formation that will benefit many of the squad players. I'll break down every aspect of the team from defence and midfield to attack and the tactical advantages that nullify the obstacles mentioned earlier.

Though Chelsea beat Everton 3-0 in the FA Cup after the Champions League Final it wasn't the most convincing of wins, but there was enough to see what Hayes was trying to accomplish. Even their first game of the new season against Arsenal saw them concede three goals. So why a back three? The fundamental principles of this system allow a team to have defensive solidity while being able to afford slightly more attacking freedom between the front three players. Between having an extra central defender and attack-minded wing-backs, the three-player system can mask deficiencies that may run through the team.

But why Chelsea, you ask? The problems that were exposed by Wolfsburg, Bayern Munich and Barcelona were well documented. The full-backs were heavily targeted and the out-of-possession movement between the midfielders showed a lack of mobility when defending against fast-paced transition teams. This makes a 3-4-2-1 system a much more viable prospect for Chelsea given the current squad make-up. The core fundamental principles of a 3-4-2-1 or 3-4-3 are:

- Athletic and intelligent defenders to cover the length and width of the field
- Disciplined midfielder to shield against counter-attacks and drop into defensive cover spots
- High and wide forwards with the ability to beat defenders off the dribble and provide crosses

- Good communication between defence and midfield units to defend well

If you look at their style of play and personnel, you can identify some key players who can play a vital role in such a system and cover the aforementioned points. Maren Mjelde, Sophie Ingle, Guro Reiten, Bethany England and Erin Cuthbert are just some who could have a monumental effect given their skillsets and qualities. This also makes up for the defensive deficiencies of the full-backs, allowing them to play a much more attacking role with extra defensive cover. The illustration in *Figure 75* below maps out the general areas each position will cover and move around in.

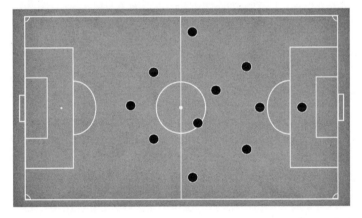

[Figure 75]

It largely remains unchanged as the front three can continue to interchange and play their natural game but now the wing-backs are encouraged to flourish and play a more attacking role while being protected.

So how does the 3-4-2-1 system break down by the thirds?

Defence

As with any tactical theory-related piece of literature, you start at the back. The first point of contention is your goalkeeper. The modern-day goalkeeper is more often than not a sweeper-keeper but the women's game is still developing those types of players. So you're almost limited to one type of them but Chelsea are quite lucky in that regard.

Chelsea's use of their keeper is fairly simple given that they have one of the best in world football. The limitations of not being a sweeper-keeper aside, the goalkeeper remains their last line of defence, bailing out the back four when teams penetrate through. Chelsea will continue to adopt this strategy and with a back three, there could be fewer shots faced by the keeper.

When analysing and transitioning to a new system, its composition becomes the first point of note. In this instance, it will be moving from two to three central defenders and playing two wing-backs as opposed to full-backs. The back three is made up of two wider centre-backs and one central one. While two centre-backs maintain their partnership and chemistry, correctly picking the third player becomes vitally important. There are two ways to go about this. Either a full-back is converted into a wider central defender or a defensive midfielder is transformed into a central centre-back. The two wing-backs can be a bit more experimental because of the added protection given by the presence of the third centre-back and double-pivot.

Building out from the back is probably the easiest role to carry out considering the strengths of their players are in ball possession, passing and control. To recap, one of the defensive midfielders will drop into space to offer a passing option but they also drop into the full-back positions to allow them to push forward. The resulting effect is to give them a chance to play long diagonal passes into the channels while allowing the full-backs to push forward to create overloads. When Sophie Ingle has played in midfield, she's dropped back into a centre-back position to allow one of the central defenders to step forward and create a better passing angle.

Given Chelsea's desire to play in the half-spaces, using three central defenders will enable them to create more effective positional rotations. With three centre-backs in play, Chelsea will naturally have space to push forward and bypass high presses. Two centre-backs can disperse into space to create a wider pitch and by adding in the defensive midfielder, there are more than enough players to create space. When one central defender steps out with the ball to start attacks, it should prompt a defensive midfielder to drop and create a passing option. However, this also enables the opposite wing-back to become free and this switch of play can open up space further forward. This is the added bonus of having a third defender to contribute in the attacking third and become another creative outlet. A quicker, more agile defender can cover the wider centre-backs, allowing them to become more creative. Aniek Nouwen might be young but has the ability to play this role and be the difference at the back.

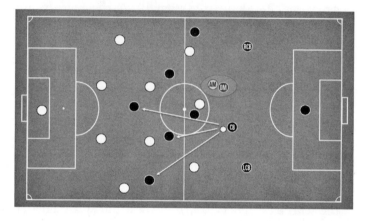

[Figure 76]

Figure 76 is an illustration of how the central defender can be a key player in Chelsea's back three in the build-up with one midfielder moving across to mark the opposition number 10 and the centre-backs stretching the pitch.

Defensively, Chelsea will again benefit from numerical superiority at the back. Given how Chelsea were at times overrun when teams penetrated their defence, there seemed to be a scramble to stop these players from taking shots. In the 2019/20 season, Chelsea averaged 6.93 shots against versus 7.21 in 2020/21. Even their expected goals against (xGA) increased from 0.72 to 0.91. So the frequency of shots faced increased which coincided with an increase in xGA. Teams were creating better goalscoring chances against this Chelsea defence and though we've seen that the issues are coming from midfield, there are obvious benefits to having three at the back.

Each centre-back and wing-back can double up and stop teams playing in the channels, and by adding in the defensive midfielder, Chelsea's swarming pressing tactics can become more effective. Taking a closer look at *Figure 77*, we see the central defender and wing-back have to be positionally aware and ensure that players don't pull them out of the highlighted zone. If teams can be shown inside, then Chelsea can use several players to close down and win back possession. The only downside is if the wing-back is moved too centrally, then the opposition full-back can overlap and create a crossing opportunity.

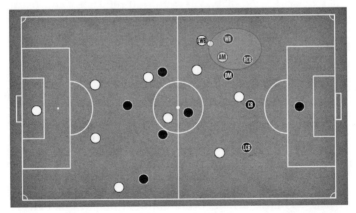

[Figure 77]

Chelsea have several options to create a well-rounded defensive line-up, and given that the qualities of their players lie on the ball rather than off it, they would be better off in adopting a quicker, possession-based build-out pattern to create a quick transition from back to front. The pace of the front three is devastating as it is, but this can become much smoother if the back three can get the ball out quicker.

Midfield

The base of a good 3-4-2-1 revolves around the double-pivot that operates to provide an attacking and defending pendulum. They act as a conduit to facilitate attacking and defensive transitions which means the two players must be vigilant and proactive in their positioning and movement.

We often see teams that play in this system include a deep-lying playmaker and box-to-box midfielder, but for Chelsea's style of play, I would argue that a top team needs to find a combination that brings both attacking and defensive qualities. A defensive-minded progressor and a dynamic box-to-box playmaker would suit this double-pivot given the attacking talent around them. However, where Chelsea are concerned they don't have the necessary ingredients to concoct a standard pairing, rather they possess the inverse.

Before elaborating on that, let's assess the current profiles. Their midfielders are a mix of box-to-box players and advanced playmakers. At the time of writing, Chelsea do not possess a specialist defensive-minded midfielder who can anchor things. Another specialist option is Ingle but her lack of mobility means she might just be better suited to playing in the back three. With no real defensive-minded player who is active in the covering phase, Chelsea might need to seek a new player from the transfer market or find an unorthodox in-house option to solve this issue.

Chelsea can use a progressive playmaking 'destroyer' – an aggressive lynchpin in the double-pivot – to complement a more box-to-box player bringing the balance. The player should possess the intelligence and proactiveness in movement and provide horizontal cover but also act as a connector between midfield and attack through progressive carries and passes. Chelsea might not have a conventional playmaker and box-to-box midfielder combination that works in this system but these proposed profiles might represent a perfect representation of what their midfield needs.

With the rotations coming from the playmaking centre-back by stepping into midfield, this defensive midfielder can shuttle across the midfield area acting as both recycler and defensive cover. This empowers her midfield partner to create or progress from deep, while also giving the wing-backs the freedom to bomb forward. This player's responsibility will be to cover the spaces in behind.

The wing-backs benefit from this system the most. Chelsea's full-back options aren't very defensively minded – Maren Mjelde being the exception – but as wing-backs, they seem to be better suited. There are comparisons that can be made here to the way Antonio Conte and Thomas Tuchel have used Marcos Alonso, Callum Hudson-Odoi and Victor Moses. All three have their vulnerabilities defensively (given the latter two are converted wingers) but they have seen their best games in a wing-back system. Equally, Chelsea can take advantage of a similar system.

Considering Chelsea's use of the half-spaces and their want to drift into the interior channels, they could adopt the use of a sort of asymmetrical attacking structure with one wing-back staying wide while the other comes inside. The way they attack in their current system would be similar, but the way the wing-backs would interact and move would change. A player like Mjelde would move into the interior channels while Guro Reiten, Jonna Andersson or Jorja Fox would instead dominate the wide spaces and benefit from a switch of play. Mjelde's presence in midfield could help shore up the centre of the pitch, adding in an extra layer of protection.

This asymmetrical tandem would give Chelsea an unpredictability in build-up and attacking patterns. Alternatively, they could do this on the left by playing Niamh Charles as the attacking wing-back on the right and have a more defensive option at left wing-back. Their current wing-back options include Charles, Andersson, Mjelde, Fox and Reiten. This system could suit Charles and Andersson to a tee given their attacking exploits and athleticism.

If we look at *Figure 78* then we'll see how an asymmetrical build-up using the wing-backs in tandem can offer a viable solution to open up space. If the ball is situated at the right wing in an overload, Chelsea can easily switch play and allow the left wing-back to push into the vacant space for a quick cross. This is something Manchester City

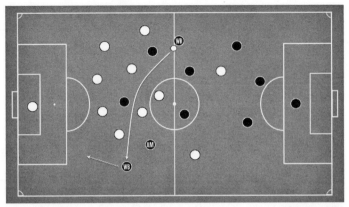

[Figure 78]

have adopted under Gareth Taylor using Lucy Bronze and Demi Stokes. The exchange of information between the men's and women's setup means Taylor has been able to discuss these tactics with Pep Guardiola's coaching staff and pick up the nuances that are used by the Spaniard. A clear example from Guardiola's team is in his use of João Cancelo as an inverted full-back. Similarly, Chelsea could do well to follow a similar path in this system.

Alternatively, when the wing-backs fly forward, they can provide the width. Though Chelsea play narrower in the final third, having the option to attack the wide spaces, stretch defences, and supply crosses is a sufficient secondary plan. To cover the spaces behind, the deepest midfielder can cover the space of the full-back that pushes forward, which emphasises the importance of the second midfielder.

This gives them licence to operate further forward and given the wing-backs' natural attacking talent, this seems a perfect fit. Taking this example in *Figure 79* from

Chelsea's final against Barcelona, the full-backs can be seen higher up the pitch with the defensive midfielder (Ingle) holding a central position. Barcelona are playing their way out from the back though there is some pressure from the forwards as the ball goes out towards Aitana Bonmatí. The second midfielder – Cuthbert – is ready and then pushes up and tracks Bonmatí's run.

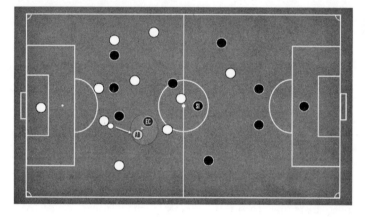

[Figure 79]

The midfielder can apply enough pressure on the player who is then forced to pass the ball back towards her own goal. An aggressive press can cause teams to restart their moves or turn over possession. Though this wasn't in a 3-4-2-1 system, there are principles from the current system that can be transferred across. The defensive midfielder is the most important component of this system and is the answer to keeping Chelsea's balance.

A midfield double-pivot has its clear advantages in numerical superiority over a single pivot. This negates the opposing team's ability to man-mark the single-pivot when playing out from the back. The use of two midfielders means there are opportunities to create space through off-the-ball movement by pulling players away. Occupation of space and opposition movement can be used to the team's advantage because a midfielder's movement into one area can drag a player away, opening space in other areas. While this is something more prevalent in the attacking third, this concept can easily be applied in build-up. With competent, creative and intellectual players playing at the base of midfield and defence, it makes passing and movement patterns much more dynamic and fluid.

Though Chelsea can use this progressive midfielder in a deeper position, the hybrid box-to-box midfielder needs to be proficient at ball distribution and positional awareness. She must also be tactically adept with an ability to read the game. They are the heartbeat of the team, controlling the game, using a range of passes, directing play from midfield, and spreading play wide. They also need to be able to cover defensively, with the onus on this player to dictate play and supply the forward line. Whether this is on the ball or off the ball, their intelligence in both scenarios needs to be high. When you watch other teams play with a double-pivot, you notice that one midfielder is much more energetic and covers a lot of ground while also proving to be a link player for the front line, as shown in *Figure 80*.

This illustration shows the movement patterns governed by the pairing, with the more attack-minded player occupying both the central pockets and space between the

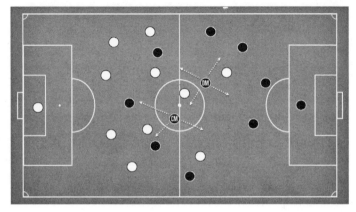

[Figure 80]

lines. Amandine Henry and Ingrid Engen are exemplary at this for Olympique Lyonnais and Wolfsburg (Engen has since moved to Barcelona) respectively.

Ji So-yun has been the go-to player in Chelsea's system as the primary playmaker, but for all her creativity, the South Korean's off-the-ball work offsets the balance of the side that makes it easier for better possession-based sides to bypass her and play around the South Korean. Ji works best as a number 10 or part of a three-player midfield where she has the freedom to roam and create.

Take the trio of Bonmatí, Alexia Putellas and Kheira Hamroaui that ran Chelsea's midfield ragged despite it being a three v three. Bonmatí and Putellas were the base of everything that Barcelona did well in combination with the front three starting with the press, and at times outplaying them in a two v three situation because of smart movements. Lluís Cortés targeted Ji as the one to press and the plan worked with the three midfielders being instructed to pressure her at every opportunity. This active movement ensured Barcelona were on top of the midfield battle.

Chelsea's box-to-box player needs to have dynamic space occupation which means the player has to take up smart pockets of space which can both benefit the team in opening up space to receive and alleviate pressure, and also with room to push forward. When an opposition number 10 and centre-forward are closing down a centre-back and defensive midfielder, the box-to-box player has to move across into space to drag one of them away, opening up space behind her position. This should prompt one of Chelsea's number 10s to drop into space and pick up possession. This method is called 'coordinated movement' where players move into each other's spaces. It's a constant movement into different positions previously vacated by another player.

If progression comes from the midfielders, then this player has the on-the-ball skills to progress the ball forward and use dynamic dribbling to create space by attracting markers towards her. This also disrupts the opposition player positions that open up space for the front three to move into. Consequently, this player can contribute and provide extra support in the final third, contributing towards the over- and under-loads that Chelsea inevitably will create. This brings the wing-back, attacking midfielder and central midfielder into play.

Attack

This now transitions us into the attacking third and how the front three will operate. In some sense, this is what the whole system was built around. Instead of talking about the theory behind each position, it makes sense to dive into the players' roles and abilities since the front three is hardly going to be a surprise. Servicing and facilitating the forwards is the basis of this operation in how to get the most out of the Pernille Harder, Sam Kerr and Fran Kirby. Hayes's understanding of how the front three work on an individual level plays off each other. The trinity of Kerr, Kirby and Harder was one of the most dynamic and devastating in world football and given how effective they were in the number of goals they scored, there is no reason to change this.

The use of a 3-4-2-1 means there is a presence of two number 10s. Though Harder and Kirby are number 9s who can play across the front line, their attributes are perfectly suited to be played as central attacking midfielders. Kerr is a very mobile striker who drifts into the left half-space and makes runs in behind. This means she likes to make a lot of diagonal runs off the shoulder of defenders, finding space between the full-back and centre-back. Kirby was the best off-the-ball attacker of the front three, with her runs in behind the opposite side full-back being a constant sight.

Any crosses that came in off the left were met by Kirby ghosting in off the right. Equally, she was adept at dropping into pockets of space between the lines and picking up possession there to become a creative source to play in Kerr and Harder. Harder has traditionally been a number 9 but has nominally played as an attacking midfielder for Chelsea last season, but can be best described as a '9.5'. Part of her role has been to drop into pockets in central midfield and be a link between midfield and attack, creating overloads and underloads in and around the half-spaces.

In the 4-4-2 system and its variations, the front three shoehorned in seemed to create awkward movements with Harder playing in one of the wider midfield roles but constantly wanting to come infield. The front two would prefer to play off someone else which left no real focal point. Though there were moments when Hayes played a 4-4-2 diamond which saw Harder move to the tip of the diamond playing off a wider front two, it did make the front three a lot more compatible, but this left the overall system feel congested. Harder wants to drop into the spaces Ji and Melanie Leupolz want to occupy in midfield, which means there's a clash of bodies. Despite Harder achieving excellent defensive numbers, she still needs space to operate in and dictate play in the final third if she is to continue as the team's number 10.

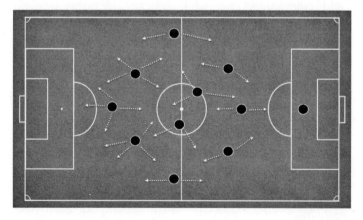

[Figure 81]

Figure 81 depicts the movement patterns of the front three but notice the space where Harder wants to go and Ji occupies. Both are overlapping and given how they're both tasked with similar creative roles in different positions, it causes an unnecessary waste of a player's skillset. Moving to a front three will not only eradicate any congested spaces but also allow the two number 10s to use the width of the pitch to create and move into. There are different variations of movement the front three can have in combination with midfield runners and wing-back movements. There is much more scope for creativity and space to rotate. I believe there will be more positional rotations between the front three in the 2021/22 season, especially since each of them is a proficient reader of the game and intelligent in their movement. Harder will be critical in glueing this team together going forward.

The space between the midfielders may now look a little less log-jammed. Harder would drop into pockets of space and not interfere with the playmaker's space. Both Kirby and Harder should be much freer to occupy spaces between the lines and attack the backline with more movement of players around them, thus creating the aforementioned overloads and underloads.

'What looks like a bizarre and possibly dysfunctional line-up on paper works beautifully because Emma Hayes has a genius understanding of how individual tendencies and stylistic attributes play off of each other to create beneficial movement and interplay,' said Om Arvind.

There is also the notion of introducing an alternative striking option in a more static focal point. Not a traditional target man, but a profile of a player who can hold up the ball and also provide a run in behind. This player can also leverage the use of the wing-backs through crosses if their primary plan is being thwarted and also because of the long diagonal balls from the back line. Being able to provide an aerial threat becomes a useful option and one that Chelsea could look to exercise more in 2021/22 to negate top-tier sides. Particularly when attacking low blocks or chasing a lead, this is an excellent choice. Chelsea ranked second after Manchester City in average crosses per 90 minutes (18.81 vs 20.11) and this only emphasises the point of having a real focal point in the forward areas.

Theoretically, Chelsea could easily execute this system with the squad that they have while still keeping to their principles of possession-based football. Weaknesses can be masked and some players can significantly be improved and leveraged for their strengths. It's how this group can adapt to the perils of knockout football that their true test will lie. And the WSL is only going to be more competitive given the recruitment of Arsenal, Manchester City and Everton, so squad rotation will be vital. Alternatively, not every season will see them be so lucky with injuries. They lost Eriksson, Bright and Mjelde for parts of the previous season and coped with their injuries, but we saw the effect the Norwegian's absence had towards the end of the campaign. We know that Chelsea's intense training regimen means fringe players are close to match-fit, but throwing them into a game state is a whole different matter. Hayes will be better off using her entire squad to maximise their value, ensure their best players are at peak physical fitness, and feel the pressure of competition. How would this team look on paper? The next chapter will discuss my choices over who should be starting and provide an alternate 11 to show depth.

17

The Eleven

THIS CHELSEA squad has a variety of profiles that could help fill the gaps in this proposed system. Given that they would need to dip into the transfer market to improve in certain areas, I suggest that they instead use some of the fringe members of the squad. The players are experienced, malleable and fluid, with versatility that can prove to be vital when it comes to adapting to a new system. Knowing what we want from this Chelsea team will bring an application to the theory. While some positions and roles are obvious fits, there are some that require more explanation so we'll elaborate here on certain positions and why they're the logical choice.

Goalkeeper: Ann-Katrin Berger

In Ann-Katrin Berger, Chelsea have one of the top three goalkeepers in football. Her performances in the 2020/21 season helped bail Chelsea out of a lot of tricky situations with her shot-stopping as a standout feature. She's also very aggressive and commanding in the box, so she isn't afraid of stopping crosses or set pieces. You need your goalkeeper to be confident and someone who can control her defence, and Berger is that player. The German shot-stopper ranked fifth for prevented goals per 90 minutes in the Women's Super League. Considering she wouldn't face as many shots as the rest of the league, this makes the statistic much more impressive. The level of concentration required to prevent goals across a 90-minute spell is high and being called into action sparingly means she needs to be proactive.

Right wing-back: Maren Mjelde

Maren Mjelde's return will be a huge boost for Emma Hayes's side this season and her jack-of-all-trades will be hugely beneficial in whatever position she plays. Playing Mjelde as a right-sided wing-back could be the next step in her career. There is no doubt that Chelsea will need fresher legs in the wing-back area; however, using her as a half-back or inverted wing-back could prove pivotal. Out of possession, if she moves into the interior channels, she can add an extra body in midfield and help stop counter-attacks higher up the pitch.

In possession, Mjelde can also be a progressive playmaker by stepping up into midfield and distributing passes. The Norwegian is very comfortable with the ball at her feet and having the cover of a defensive midfielder around her can indeed afford her more space to operate in. Mjelde is in the 85th percentile of progressive carries for full-backs at an average of 6.00 per 90 minutes. Though

Chelsea use progressive passes as a main source of build-up, this is definitely more viable in breaking high-pressing teams. Defensively, she'll be able to read the game and cover vacant spaces facilitating better attacking patterns.

Central centre-back: Aniek Nouwen

Probably an option for the future, Aniek Nouwen could be a long-term solution as the central centre-back for Chelsea. Nouwen is a technically gifted yet physically powerful central defender with the best years of her career ahead of her. At 22, Nouwen is vastly experienced, having made over 100 appearances for PSV as well as winning 14 caps for the Netherlands. Her role as a centre-back is more of a sweeper than a stopper. She possesses pace and agility that ensures any movement or passes behind the defensive line are covered using a combination of intelligence and positional play.

Nouwen uses physicality and intelligent tackling to win back possession and is especially good at one-on-one defending, which makes her positioning vitally important. A defender's foundation is based on good positioning which can be leveraged in most situations, especially on the counter-attack. We know that Chelsea's problems come in the half-space transitions but one-on-one defending is also deemed an issue, especially when counter-attacked. Even if she isn't successful at dispossessing the player, she should have enough to delay the attacking move.

Her biggest asset is her body orientation and positioning to cover the space behind the defensive line and her partner.

Her intelligence at such a young age is sublime, especially out of possession that will allow Eriksson and Bright to play more aggressively beside her. Given the fluid movement of most forward lines, being a sweeper is much more important than it ever was. Being able to anticipate, cover and then dispossess the opposition is critical.

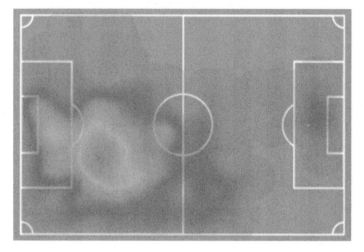

[Figure 82]

Nouwen's heat map in *Figure 82* mirrors what's been discussed, which is heavy movement in her own box. Her most active areas indicate a player that previously played for a side that doesn't hold a very high line so she was used to defending slightly deeper and engaging in more defensive duels when she was at PSV Eindhoven.

The Dutch international averaged 10.14 interceptions and 4.6 clearances per 90 minutes across the Eredivisie and UEFA Women's Champions League this season, which indicates her ability to anticipate rather than lunge into challenges. In 763 minutes, Nouwen had not received a single booking, which is mightily impressive and points towards her discipline and accuracy in defending.

Nouwen's ability on the ball isn't short of quality either. As a defender, she is comfortable and assured in possession, as well as being press-resistant. Given how most teams play a very intense, high-pressing strategy at the highest level, this trait makes her all the more desirable.

As part of this back three, Nouwen's role will be to defend and provide a base for the wider central defenders to defend as stoppers, acting as an insurance policy. Being reliable on the ball is a minimum requirement but much of the passing will be overseen by Eriksson and Bright. Her injection of pace would be much needed and learning from two of the best centre-backs will only accelerate her development. Will she be prone to mistakes? Yes, but if she is deemed good enough for Chelsea then playing in most games will only help her improve.

Central midfielder: Melanie Leupolz

With the risk of repeating myself and explaining what Melanie Leupolz's skillset is, I will elaborate on my reasons for her inclusion as part of the double-pivot. The German's attributes are perfectly suited to Chelsea's style of play. She is arguably the most balanced midfielder at Chelsea with a mixture of positional awareness, ball recycling and vision. The midfielder would play slightly further forward, but because of the way Chelsea need their double-pivot to play, both Leupolz and her partner will not be too distant from each other. Her main role will be to service the front three and provide the pass that starts the attacking move while also providing defensive assuredness, adding bite and solidity to the midfield which is part of the double-pivot's responsibilities.

During the first week of the WSL, Arsenal head coach Jonas Eidevall talked about Chelsea's frailties when teams will force the issue and go on to them, leaving Chelsea exposed in transition. Though Leupolz struggled against Arsenal, it came down to being new to the system but also needing the right partner to create that balance.

'Leupolz is a really underrated player in the midfield. She's a box-to-box midfielder who's really good at breaking play, getting the ball back and starting a quick attack and with her vision she plays that smart pass forward,' said Alex Ibaceta.

Left wing-back: Guro Reiten

Guro Reiten has started the season as Chelsea's first-choice left wing-back and has thrived so far in the role. When playing three at the back, teams can afford to utilise attack-minded wing-backs given the defence-heavy nature of the system. Reiten is an excellent winger and has shown proficiency in servicing and supplying Chelsea's forwards in her minutes further up the pitch.

Part of the reason to have someone like her play at left wing-back is to give Chelsea an extra player in the final third and an alternate option of attack. Given the side's natural instinct to attack the central and interior channels, using Reiten on the left as a wider option gives them a way of being unpredictable.

Though Jonna Andersson is the most natural fit in terms of the position, Reiten has already shown that she is capable of competing. The Norwegian winger uses her pace, skill and crossing to attack and has decent positional awareness. Beating opposition full-backs will be key and is the one skill that stands out for Reiten. We know that Harder will want to cut inside so the overlapping combinations will be extremely complementary, but also vastly different to the way Chelsea will use the right flank.

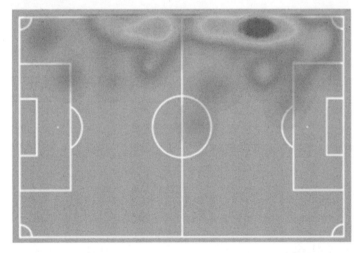

[Figure 83]

The heat map in *Figure 83* is based on her first two games of the current WSL season and while the sample size is very small, it gives us an early indication of the positions she wants to take up. Games against Arsenal and Everton show that Reiten is extremely active in the final third but has been equally prevalent at defending. Most of her movements are wide which also supports the notion of being the overlapping player and forming the balance across both flanks. If we go by the theory from the previous chapter, we want one side to adopt a wider position while the other stays a bit narrower.

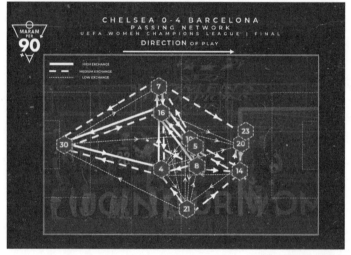

[Figure 84]

Realistically, we'll see teething problems against top sides considering the position is new to her but there is potential for Reiten to become a well-rounded wing-back. Just like *Figure 84* depicts, the full-backs were balanced in their approach and the same idea can be applied to this back-three system where Reiten can be the one pushing up from the left. The role allows her the attacking freedom but also takes advantage of her pace and positioning to carry out her defensive duties. Reiten can learn the position over time and stake her claim as the first-choice player. The proposed system allows for at least one side to be attacking and who better to play the position than one of Chelsea's best attacking wide players?

Defensive midfielder: Jessie Fleming

Jessie Fleming is arguably the one player every Chelsea fan wants to see given more game time. This season should see the gold medallist secure more game time given her Olympic exploits. For our system, Fleming could be the perfect mould to complete the double-pivot and assume the role of a defensive-minded box-to-box midfielder.

The 23-year-old is a central midfielder that has the makings of becoming an excellent box-to-box midfielder. Fleming's playing style is very much that of a progressive ball carrier who has excellent spatial awareness with a raw ability to marshal a midfield. She can dribble and ghost past players with ease and has very close control which enables her to keep possession of the ball. The ability to become a progressive dribbler means she doesn't need an elaborative range of passing and given the expected high press from opposing teams, this gives Chelsea a very good alternate progression option. Her simple and effective passes are more than enough because she can move into good positions through her movement with the ball. We saw glimpses of potential during her run with Canada where she was dropping her shoulder to outmuscle her marker, evade pressing players, and facilitate ball progression, all by dribbling past players as if they weren't there.

She has the ability to increase the tempo and play quicker if required. This brings us to another important aspect of her game – her ability to pick up possession on the turn. Her first touch and comfort in receiving passes under pressure enable her progressive role. Receiving in deeper positions means she can easily bridge the gap between the advanced wide centre-back and the forwards. There's an element of Amandine Henry in Fleming in that they both have an uncanny ability to ghost past players with ease from midfield and provide a threat going forward while being defensively savvy. Chelsea have one of the best progressive midfielders in world football if given regular game time and a chance to flourish. We saw against Barcelona how much the Catalan midfielders affected the game out of possession, so the combination of Fleming and Leupolz could improve Chelsea's midfield in that aspect. Fleming isn't the best tackler but her aggression and proactiveness off the ball means she can harass opposition players to win back possession through pressure and misplaced passes.

'As Canada receded and played for penalties, Fleming's work against the ball became more and more important. By extra time, she had gone from making the occasional recovery run and tackle to constantly facing up versus the likes of Kosovare Asllani and Jonna Andersson,' said Om Arvind.

'The skill, intensity and awareness present in Fleming's defensive work were a coach's dream and reminiscent of the type of Mikkel Damsgaard-esque completeness that allows number 10s to survive in the modern era.'

Yes, Fleming is a number 10 by virtue of her position but she has the skillset to play deeper. Playing in this double-pivot, Fleming can provide both a method of progression through build-up from deep but she can equally use her spatial awareness to move into good positions off the ball. Her intelligence in being a passing option cannot be underestimated as it aids in space creation. We know that this system is predicated on how well the midfielders operate off the ball as much as on it. She gives you an all-round presence without stepping on the attackers' toes. *Figure 85* is her heat map which depicts her average movement patterns from the 2020/21 season. You can see how she is effectively playing in the right half-space and rarely occupies the central areas.

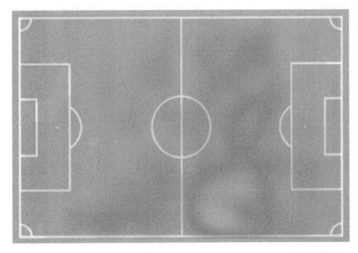

[Figure 85]

Though she played 1,322 minutes for club and country last season, for comparison's sake, we'll look at the top 30-ranked players to see where she averages. Fleming registered 5.47 passes to the final third per 90 minutes (Fleming's WSL minutes are 494). The 30th-ranked player in the WSL averaged 6.72 passes to the final third per 90 across 1,741 minutes. Even though there is a gulf, we can see that Fleming is attempting to progress the ball as frequently as possible. Similarly, the 30th-ranked player averages 2.06 progressive runs per 90 across 1,091 minutes with Fleming averaging 0.73 per 90. It's tough to do any statistical comparison at this time but the point is to show that Fleming is attempting these progression methods and will improve on these numbers as she is granted more minutes on the pitch.

If she can provide even half of the effect Henry or Mateo Kovačić have given to their respective teams, then Chelsea will have one of the best progressive midfielders in world football. Fleming is one player who needs to be playing regular first-team football this season and by the time you read this chapter, she might well be doing so.

Notable alternatives
Centre-forward: Bethany England
While Bethany England wasn't Chelsea's first-choice striker in 2020/21, the England international still brings a different profile and variation to the team. In the previous chapter we discussed and talked about having a focal point, a player who can play with their back to goal but also

make runs in behind while being more disciplined in her positioning and movement in a sense. While Sam Kerr is an excellent striker, we have seen Chelsea needing to come up with answers to break down stubborn, low-block teams. Even when they blew away many a team, there were times when an alternative idea could have been more beneficial.

England presents this option with her pace, understanding of space, and ability to know how to score goals. She was the second-highest goalscorer two seasons ago (14), where she displayed an excellent, well-rounded game. She also brings an aerial threat which makes floated crosses much more of a viable option when chasing games. Additionally, it suits the direct style that Chelsea are known to use.

Defensive midfielder: Erin Cuthbert

This is probably where I play my wildcard and mention Erin Cuthbert as an alternative option for a defensive midfielder. Cuthbert has the ability and skillset to become a tenacious defensive midfielder who patrols the deeper areas, protecting the back four. She's a natural wide player who can play a more central role because her aggressive style can be transferred into a different position. In Cuthbert, Chelsea have a player who can become an aggressive lynchpin in the double-pivot that can complement a more creative player.

Cuthbert has the skills of a dynamic box-to-box midfielder who can be the team's shuttler and move across the pitch giving horizontal cover. It would be interesting to see Cuthbert offer a viable solution to the 'destroyer' role, playing deeper while providing some forward drive.

With the rotations coming from the playmaking centre-back, Cuthbert can shuttle across the defensive midfield area acting as both recycler and defensive cover by dropping into the spaces vacated by the centre-back and wing-backs. This also empowers her midfield partner to create or progress from deep, as well as giving the wing-backs the freedom to bomb forward. Cuthbert can solely focus on covering the spaces vacated by the full-backs.

This is further emphasised in Cuthbert's defensive data where she's averaged 23.3 pressures per 90 minutes with 10.6 coming in the middle third as well as 3.42 tackles per 90. This is arguably the most transformative change Chelsea can make if they decide not to dip into the transfer market for a specialist option. Cuthbert may not have the positional discipline to be a ready-made solution right now, but with coaching and time, she could develop this part of her game and become an extremely important option.

Any combination of the three midfielders would work against top-quality opposition while allowing the front three to flourish. The reason behind having the Fleming/ Leupolz double-pivot is to bring energy, aggressiveness and progressive carries from midfield. In theory, their skillsets should offer something different but in reality, it will take time to adapt and adjust. Cuthbert is liable to positional lapses but playing her in such a vital position could possibly help accelerate her improvement in this position. At the end of the day, it permits Chelsea to offer an alternative tactical solution.

[Figure 86]

Figure 86 is what I think the Chelsea team should look like under the aforementioned system. Playing in a 3-4-2-1 does not only complement the current set of players but it gives Chelsea a better way of balancing defence and attack. With a few tweaks, this formation could play into their hands and make it difficult for teams to break them down, especially in the latter stages of the UEFA Women's Champions League.

* * *

This system and team could do well under the circumstances and considering how Hayes thinks she can improve the squad further without the need for further signings, it illustrates her trust and ability to improve the current set of players. This starting 11 has a good mix of experience, youth and most importantly, cohesion between the thirds. The midfield seems more balanced and less inclined to want to step into each third's vicinity to the point of conflict.

The depth in each position is another important factor. The additions of Lauren James and Aniek Nouwen only add to this and brings an even younger feel to the rotation group and the return of Mjelde from injury will help significantly. Though more signings should be made – especially in key positions such as full-back – these players could yet still make an impact and give Chelsea an alternative in a season that will have up to three contenders for the WSL as well as a host of them in the UEFA Women's Champions League.

18

Can Chelsea Eclipse Lyon and Barcelona?

NINETY MINUTES seemed like an eternity for Chelsea. Once the final whistle blew in Gothenburg, there was a sense of relief for the Chelsea players as much as there was jubilation for Barcelona. Their defining moment to shine on the biggest stage in front of the world was shattered by a rampant Barcelona side who themselves felt the same pain two years earlier. The hollow, empty stadium was chilling with the players wanting to seclude themselves from the rest of the world. Their opponents had been there before and it was a stark reminder to Emma Hayes and Chelsea that they are a short way off the summit.

* * *

There's one moment you can pinpoint in every dominant team's history as the one that began their ascent to the top of the mountain. The Champions League Final loss to Barcelona is a significant one, not just in terms of defeat but also as a moment that could push Chelsea to become an even better version of themselves. It put Hayes in a new position to try and improve her team to get to the next level. History tells us she's a willing learner and a motivator. Her man-management abilities have been impeccable, but it will surely be tested now having to lift the team and get them to believe they can become the best in Europe.

Nick Verlaney explained, 'Emma Hayes is one of football's truly bright lights. Having briefly met her and watched her run a training session during the 2016/17 season at Cobham, she is all of these things: tough, demanding, empathetic, charismatic, whip-smart, funny, engaging, etc. But what stood out to me, and other *London Is Blue Podcast* boys, was that she walked the [sic] talk. She's a servant leader, which is all too rare these days. There's no doubt that all of these qualities make up her leadership style, but the fact that she's willing to go the extra mile, to find new sports science methodology that suits her players to use one example, contributes to what she really is at her core: a winner. Never mind the ten trophies in her cabinet. Winning is a state of mind. It's her state of mind. And it rubs off on everyone around her.'

There's a similar storyline in that Barcelona were thrashed by Lyon but then used it as a platform to build from. They rallied together and made a run for the trophy in just two seasons. Chelsea can take many lessons of their own from the way Barcelona conducted themselves in that time. Barcelona had been in two semi-finals and a final before finally winning the crown. For Chelsea, with two

Women's Super League titles in back-to-back seasons, there is still much encouragement to be had for Hayes's side.

The Catalans are currently the best club side in the world while Olympique Lyonnais, Paris Saint Germain, Bayern Munich and Wolfsburg will all surely make a triumphant return in the 2021/22 UEFA Women's Champions League. Lyon set the tone for European dominance while Barcelona look set to take over the mantle; it will be up to Hayes to find a way to navigate Chelsea to the top. This now feels like the start of another project, but do Chelsea have what it takes to become the next European powerhouse club? Can they beat the likes of Barcelona and Lyon this season?

Alex Ibaceta offered, 'Chelsea got lucky in the lead-up vs Wolfsburg, Atleti and Bayern. Yes, they played okay and managed to win the game, but if Atleti scored those penalties it could've been different, if Wolfsburg put away the 100 chances that they created or if Bayern scored the chances they had in the last minutes of the semi-final it would've been completely different. They have undeniably one of the best squads in the world, but their lead-up to the final definitely didn't reflect that, I found. And in the final you got to see which team was better prepared.'

The answer lies somewhere in between. Do they have the capability to do it? Yes. But it comes down to managing the finer details across 180 minutes of knockout football. Chelsea ended their ties better than they started them, and these teams will punish them for it if there's a repeat again in 2021/22.

Lyon, Paris Saint-Germain and Wolfsburg may all be starting from scratch, but their core group still remains and a positive transfer window has seen them add some excellent names to their squads. Daniëlle van de Donk and Christiane Endler joined Lyon, Wolfsburg signed Jill Roord, and Sofia Jakobsson joined Bayern Munich. Chelsea, meanwhile, added Lauren James and Aniek Nouwen, but both can be regarded as long-term signings. Hayes is confident going into the new season that she can extract more out of her current crop of players. Whether additions need to be made in January remains to be seen but there are enough fringe players who could come in to make a difference.

'It's again, that under-appreciation of [Barcelona] doing all the basics so good. It's the Barcelona philosophy and improved at that. If everyone thought Pep's Barça were the best, the level of excellence of this team is equally the same looking from a football perspective,' said Ibaceta.

There is no doubt this squad has the makings of contributing to long-term success. Though it seems like they are some way behind Barcelona in terms of efficiency, it only takes a few tweaks to turn the tide. Will they win this edition of the UEFA Women's Champions League? There's a strong possibility because you would imagine Hayes has learnt from last season's journey. If the foundations are set correctly, then it can catapult the team to atmospheric heights for years to come. Hayes has already cemented her legacy in Chelsea and European legend, but capping it off by finally commanding a seat on the throne will validate all the years of facing uphill battles and definitively put to rest the question of if they have the makings of being Europe's next powerhouse club.